MARKETING BOOK

"Marketing is constantly changing, but the concepts explained so clearly in *The Smart Marketing Book* are timeless."

Sarah White, Senior Global Insight Manager, Britvic

"Great for those that don't want to drown in evidence but want to understand, and share, some of the most important principles in marketing."

Richard Bambrick, Senior Consumer Insight Manager, Pentland Brands

"A veritable feast of marketing ideas. Whether you're a student or a pro, Dan White has produced a smart guide to effective marketing."

Darren Bhattachary, CEO – Insights, Kantar

"With engaging visual mnemonics and clear, to-the-point copy, Dan White has demonstrated that he is a master of the art of making things simple in this useful little book."

Chuck Young, CEO, Ameritest

"*The Smart Marketing Book* is everything it sets out to be: an intelligent, comprehensive and clear review of marketing principles, each one supported by a unique summary image."

Nigel Hollis, Chief Global Brand Analyst, Kantar

"Very clearly structured and written, with new ways of presenting novel but also some well-known concepts, using witty and stylish drawings."

Dimitri Pisarsky, MD, Millward Brown A/R/M/I Marketing

"Dan White's *The Smart Marketing Book* is a perfect read for anyone entering their first role. Actually, it's a good read for more practiced marketers too. Read it – you'll pick up something new, for sure."

Duncan MacConnol, Joint Managing Director, Quantic

"I no longer have the time to pull out trusty copies of Kotler, Reis or Covey and the 'fast-food' reductiveness of many modern 'models' either leaves me cold or none the wiser as to their practical application. [This book] is appropriately sophisticated for our complex times, while somehow retaining an immediacy and pragmatism that makes me feel smarter."

Cliff Nichols, National Head of Insights and Marketing, Cox Architecture

"A helpful and informative book that (literally!) illustrates key business, marketing and consumer principles clearly ... A great introduction for anyone new to marketing, but equally, a valuable reminder and prompt for the more experienced business reader too."

Charlotte May, Group Head of Customer Research, Legal & General

"*The Smart Marketing Book* is a concentrated journey in how to practically solve an array of marketing puzzles. Dan never pretends to have all the answers. Rather, he brings wisdom and seeks to equip marketers with proven tools to help them make better day-to-day decisions."

Tim Wragg, CEO, North America Kantar

"This is a great book – it's a distillation of a career's worth of learning into something even a newcomer can understand."

David Chantrey, Transformation Director, Kantar

"I wish this book had been around when I was coming through the ranks."

Richard Clissold-Vasey, Transformation Director, Kantar

FOR OTHER TITLES IN THE SERIES...

CLEVER CONTENT, DYNAMIC IDEAS, PRACTICAL SOLUTIONS AND ENGAGING VISUALS – A CATALYST TO INSPIRE NEW WAYS OF THINKING AND PROBLEM-SOLVING IN A COMPLEX WORLD

www.lidpublishing.com/product-category/concise-advice-series

Published by
LID Publishing Limited
An imprint of LID Business Media Ltd.
LABS House, 15-19 Bloomsbury Way,
London, WC1A 2TH, UK

info@lidpublishing.com
www.lidpublishing.com

A member of:

businesspublishersroundtable.com

All rights reserved. Without limiting the rights under copyright reserved, no part of this publication may be reproduced, stored or introduced into a retrieval system, or transmitted, in any form or by any means (electronic, mechanical, photocopying, recording or otherwise) without the prior written permission of both the copyright owners and the publisher of this book.

© Dan White, 2025
© LID Publishing Limited, 2025

ISBN: 978-1-915951-71-7
ISBN: 978-1-915951-72-4 (ebook)

Cover and page design: Caroline Li

THE SMART MARKETING BOOK

**THE DEFINITIVE GUIDE TO
EFFECTIVE MARKETING STRATEGIES**

DAN WHITE

MADRID | MEXICO CITY | LONDON
BUENOS AIRES | BOGOTA | SHANGHAI

CONTENTS

INTRODUCTION viii

1 MARKETING 1
  1.1 HOW BUSINESSES MAKE MONEY 2
  1.2 PURPOSE OF MARKETING 4
  1.3 GROWTH STRATEGIES 6
  1.4 THE MARKETING MIX 8
  1.5 MARKETING'S BUSINESS PARTNERS 11

2 BRAND DEVELOPMENT 15
  2.1 HOW BRANDS EXIST IN THE BRAIN 16
  2.2 BRAND PURPOSE AND STRATEGY 19
  2.3 THE BRAND PIÑATA 22
  2.4 PRICE POSITIONING 25
  2.5 BRAND KPIs 27

3 BRAND EXPERIENCE 31
  3.1 DEFINING THE BRAND EXPERIENCE 32
  3.2 IDENTIFYING THE MOMENTS THAT MATTER 35
  3.3 CUSTOMER SERVICE EXCELLENCE 38
  3.4 HANDLING COMPLAINTS 41
  3.5 CUSTOMER MANAGEMENT SYSTEMS 44

4 INNOVATION 47
  4.1 INNOVATION STRATEGY 48
  4.2 INNOVATION PROCESS 51
  4.3 GENERATING INNOVATION IDEAS 55
  4.4 ASSESSING INNOVATION POTENTIAL 58
  4.5 LAUNCHING NEW PRODUCTS 61

5 COMMUNICATIONS 65
  5.1 HOW COMMUNICATIONS WORK 66
  5.2 USING COMMUNICATIONS TO BUILD A BRAND 69
  5.3 CHOOSING THE RIGHT TYPES OF MEDIA 72

		5.4	CHANNEL ROLES AND CONNECTIONS	77
		5.5	MEDIA PLANNING AND BUDGETING	80

6 CREATIVE CONTENT — 85
- 6.1 GENERATING A COMMUNICATIONS IDEA — 86
- 6.2 ASSESSING CREATIVE IDEAS — 89
- 6.3 ASSESSING PIECES OF CONTENT — 92
- 6.4 THE IMPORTANCE OF BRANDING — 96
- 6.5 OPTIMIZING CONTENT — 99

7 SALES PROMOTION — 103
- 7.1 WHEN TO ADJUST PRICING — 104
- 7.2 WHEN TO USE PRICE PROMOTIONS — 106
- 7.3 PROMOTIONS TO BUILD THE CUSTOMER BASE — 109
- 7.4 PROMOTIONS TO ATTRACT LAPSED BUYERS — 112
- 7.5 SCHEMES TO ENHANCE RETENTION — 115

8 MEASUREMENT — 119
- 8.1 USING DATA TO DRIVE MARKETING DECISIONS — 120
- 8.2 MEASURING BRAND PROGRESS — 123
- 8.3 MEASURING COMMUNICATIONS EFFECTIVENESS — 125
- 8.4 MEASURING CUSTOMER EXPERIENCE — 130
- 8.5 KEEPING TABS ON THE COMPETITION — 133

9 BRAND REVIEW — 137
- 9.1 REVIEWING BRAND STRATEGY — 138
- 9.2 DEVISING A NEW BRAND STRATEGY — 140
- 9.3 MARKETING PLANNING — 144
- 9.4 BUDGET SETTING — 147
- 9.5 BRAND PORTFOLIOS — 150

10 BRAND EXTENSION — 155
- 10.1 EXTENDING TO NEW CATEGORIES — 156
- 10.2 BRAND LICENSING — 159
- 10.3 SCALING TO NEW REGIONS — 162
- 10.4 INTERNATIONAL VS LOCAL COMMUNICATIONS — 165
- 10.5 LEVERAGING YOUR CORE COMPETENCIES — 169

BIBLIOGRAPHY — 172
ABOUT THE AUTHOR — 173

INTRODUCTION

Marketing is an exciting, dynamic profession requiring an unparalleled breadth of knowledge, technical understanding and creativity. Psychological discoveries and new technologies create a continual flow of marketing opportunities. With these innovations, however, come risks and considerable confusion. Marketers can feel overwhelmed by all the complexity and the new ideas they are expected to assimilate. Most marketing books add to the mental logjam by exploring a novel perspective in detail without explaining how it relates to established marketing principles. Successive fads lead marketers to hone their craft in one area at the expense of others. Few marketers have time to read overly specialist books that ignore the bigger picture.

The Smart Marketing Book is different. It brings together old and new marketing thinking, explaining in clear, succinct terms how everything connects and how it can be applied in day-to-day decision-making. Technologies and business models might be in a constant state of flux, but the workings of the brain evolve slowly. This book equips marketers with the principles and concepts they need to assimilate the new and navigate the industry's complexity with confidence.

The following ten chapters cover different aspects of marketing. Each chapter stands alone, but newcomers to the profession will find it easier to build up their knowledge by reading them in order. Ideas are conveyed in clear, accessible language, supported by frameworks – some old, some new – and brought to life by unique visualizations. The goal is for the reader to take in complex ideas with ease and become confident applying them.

The Smart Marketing Book is an indispensable guide for anyone who has taken on the fascinating challenge of building a career in marketing.

If you find this book useful and would like to to gain a deeper understanding of some of its key topics, please look out for *The Smart Branding Book* and *The Smart Advertising Book* from the same author.

PART **ONE**

THE MARKETING MIX EYE

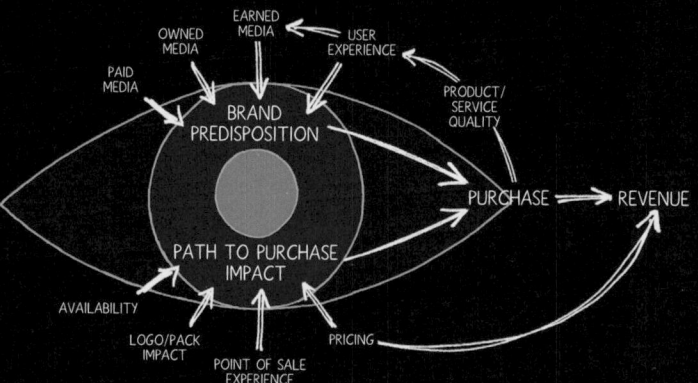

MARKETING

1.1 HOW BUSINESSES MAKE MONEY

Since most businesses exist to make money for their owners, they need to provide better returns than alternatives such as government bonds, which offer low risk and guaranteed returns. In the past few decades, bonds have yielded between 2% and 5% per year, which explains why businesses usually aim to deliver a profit significantly greater than this, often 10% or more.

The finances of a company work in the same way as those of a household. If you have more revenue coming in than costs going out, you make a profit and start accumulating cash. In business, this cash either goes to the owners/shareholders or it's invested in the business to maximize future profits.

HOW BUSINESSES MAKE MONEY

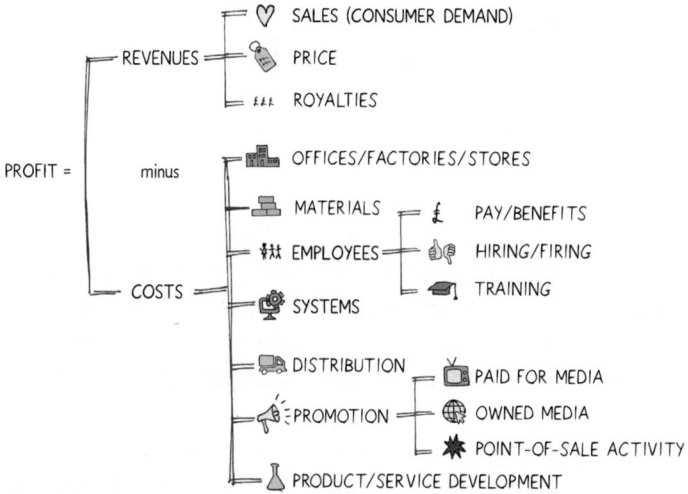

Revenues depend on the volume of products or services sold, the price at which they're sold, and any royalties received from partners selling the company's offer under licence.

Costs can arise from the need for buildings, materials, equipment and software, as well as the expense of hiring, training and paying employees. There may also be costs from transporting goods to retailers and advertising used to stimulate sales. Most companies also have ongoing costs for developing new and improved products and services required to keep the company's offer competitive.

1.2 PURPOSE OF MARKETING

There is no universal definition of marketing. It can refer to both the money-making approach adopted by a business as well as a responsibility within a business for governing the approach. In keeping with its ethos, *The Smart Marketing Book*'s definition is a succinct one:

To create, promote and deliver products or services that enable commercial objectives to be met through the customer value they generate.

This definition emphasizes marketing's responsibility for balancing the business's need to make a profit with the need for customers to be happy with what they receive for the money they pay. Effective marketing involves creating value that benefits the customer and the business.

Great marketing-led businesses are continually looking for ways to increase the gap between customer value and cost of delivery.

COMMERCIAL IMPACT OF MARKETING

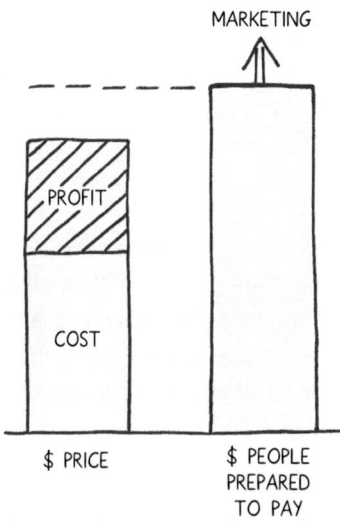

Widening the gap creates opportunities for the business. One option is to keep prices relatively low and give customers an exceptionally good deal. This will help attract more customers and generate positive reviews and recommendations, which, in turn, bring in even more customers. Alternatively, the customer value created by marketing could be used to support higher prices in order to generate greater profit. Whatever the commercial objectives of the business are, marketing can support them by maximizing customer value.

Marketing also contributes to a business by underlining why the company exists, its unique contribution to the world. The idea of a purpose beyond profit can guide a business's development, inspire employees and attract potential employees.

1.3 GROWTH STRATEGIES

The Ansoff Matrix, introduced by mathematician and business leader Igor Ansoff, highlights four options for achieving growth. The key decision is whether to scale an existing offer or develop something new. The strategy chosen governs where the company's time and money should be focused.

ANSOFF GROWTH STRATEGY MATRIX

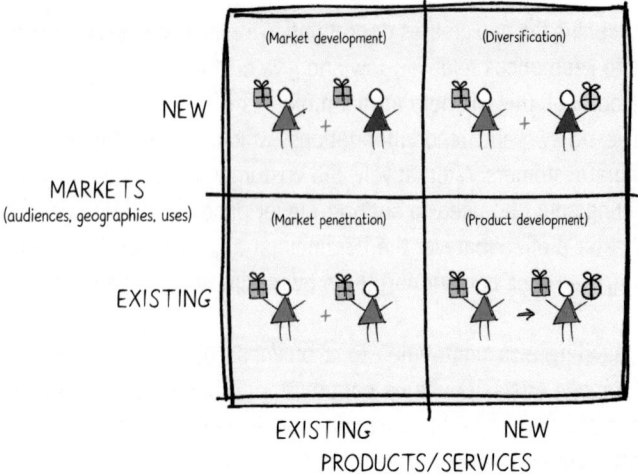

MARKET PENETRATION

This strategy is for companies with a product that is stronger than competitors but hasn't yet been discovered by much of its target audience. In other words, it still has a lot of 'headroom' for growth that could be unlocked by investing further in distribution-building, sales and marketing.

MARKET DEVELOPMENT

This is an effective strategy if the brand is reaching saturation in its current market but could replicate its success among different types of consumer or in new regions. Success depends on delivering impactful marketing activity, as well as efficient distribution to new audiences.

PRODUCT DEVELOPMENT

This is a viable strategy if existing customers have a high regard for the brand and would be receptive to new products it offers. Brands seen as trustworthy and innovative have an advantage here because people believe their new products are worth buying and tend to scrutinize them less. This explains the queues of people outside Apple stores in the 2000s waiting to buy the brand's latest gadget. For a product development strategy to succeed, the company needs enough budget to develop exciting new products that the brand's loyal customer base will snap up.

DIVERSIFICATION

This strategy is extremely rare since it is only viable if the company has the money to develop new products and expand into new regions at the same time. This only tends to occur if the company has a technology or capability that is way ahead of the curve and has plentiful financial backing.

1.4 THE MARKETING MIX

Once the growth strategy has been defined, it is put into effect by investing in the 'marketing mix.' This consists of the variables that influence how much customers value the company's products and services and can be remembered as the four, five, six or seven 'Ps' of marketing.

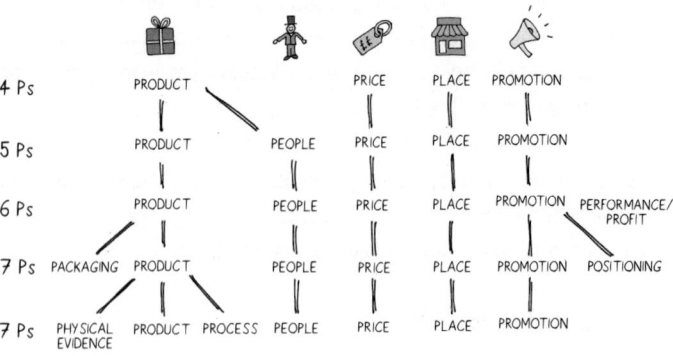

THE MANY Ps OF MARKETING

4 Ps		PRODUCT		PRICE	PLACE	PROMOTION
5 Ps		PRODUCT	PEOPLE	PRICE	PLACE	PROMOTION
6 Ps		PRODUCT	PEOPLE	PRICE	PLACE	PROMOTION / PERFORMANCE/PROFIT
7 Ps	PACKAGING	PRODUCT	PEOPLE	PRICE	PLACE	PROMOTION / POSITIONING
7 Ps	PHYSICAL EVIDENCE	PRODUCT / PROCESS	PEOPLE	PRICE	PLACE	PROMOTION

The original four Ps framework encompasses the whole mix; later versions highlight components that aren't immediately apparent from the labels of the four core areas.

The Smart Marketing Book's marketing mix framework is based on the Ps but introduces modern terminology and shows how the elements interact to influence purchasing and generate revenue.

THE MARKETING MIX EYE

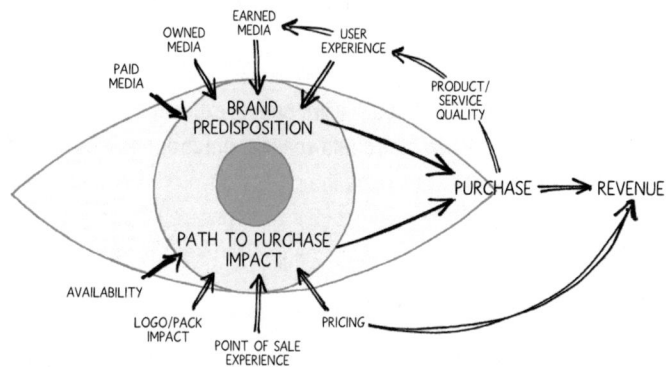

BRAND PREDISPOSITION: how inclined people are toward the brand. Higher brand predisposition means more customers are likely to buy the brand at the asking price. The term 'brand equity' is often used in a similar way to brand predisposition.

PAID MEDIA: external communications channels that have to be paid. Examples include social media, video streaming services, TV, magazines, in-store activity, paid search and sponsorship.

OWNED MEDIA: communications mechanisms owned by the company such as websites, social media profiles, subscriber newsletters and owned retail outlets.

EARNED MEDIA: positive or negative comments about the brand from third parties such as news stories, magazine articles, vlogs, customer reviews or comments in social media.

USER EXPERIENCE: how people feel about their experience of the product from a sample or after purchase. This is by far the biggest influence on brand predisposition and depends on the product or service quality delivered.

PATH TO PURCHASE IMPACT: what people experience in the run-up to a purchase decision that could make them more or less likely to buy the brand.

AVAILABILITY: how easy it is for people to find out about, try and buy the brand.

LOGO/PACK IMPACT: the ability of the logo or pack design to draw the eye and conjure positive feelings toward the brand.

POINT OF SALE EXPERIENCE: what people experience in the moments before making a purchase. This includes any price deals or other incentives being offered by the brand and competitors. These have a big impact on which brand is chosen, especially for anyone who isn't strongly predisposed to buying a particular brand.

PRICING: the price of the brand compared to alternatives. This is the acid test of how effective the marketing activities have been in creating brand disposition versus the competition so that people will buy the brand at the asking price.

1.5 MARKETING'S BUSINESS PARTNERS

For marketing to have a strong influence on the business, it needs to develop close relationships with other business units and external suppliers. This ensures that everyone is focused on delivering a user experience that meets or exceeds expectations.

MARKETING'S KEY PARTNERS

MARKET RESEARCH
Market research is marketing's closest ally, since it provides the consumer understanding needed to guide the strategy and optimize the marketing mix.

FINANCE
Marketing is one of the few investments companies consider to be optional. For established businesses especially, cutting marketing spend will not usually result in a sudden downturn in sales, but will reduce company costs and improve profits, which is why marketing budgets are often squeezed in order to hit short-term targets. However, marketing investment is vital to sustainable business success. Marketers need to provide clear evidence of the long-term return from marketing investment in order to justify and secure budget each year.

RESEARCH AND DEVELOPMENT
Marketers are responsible for guiding the company's R&D (research and development) to create new products that consumers will value. The brief should be to find unique ways of enhancing people's lives that are worth more that it would cost the company to deliver them.

CREATIVE AGENCY
The role of the creative agency is to come up with an idea, based on what's special about the brand and its products, that resonates powerfully with potential customers. This idea becomes the underlying theme reflected in all the brand's communications.

MEDIA AGENCY
The media agency's job is to find the most cost-effective ways of connecting with people in the target audience when they are receptive to hearing about what the brand has to offer.

OPERATIONS
In a perfect organization, the customer experience will live up to the marketing promise. In reality, operational limitations can result in delivery that falls short of the desired standard. Marketing and operational teams need to work closely together to ensure that customer expectations are matched consistently by what the company is able to deliver.

SALES
Marketing briefs the sales team on what to sell, whom to target and which selling messages to prioritize. Being in direct contact with customers means the salesforce soon learns what is and isn't compelling, so it pays for marketers to listen carefully to this feedback and use it to adjust the mix.

IT
Effective marketing depends increasingly on leveraging the multitude of data available on consumer behaviours and attitudes. Marketers need to know how to use this data to guide strategy and optimize marketing activities, working with IT specialists to determine how the data could be collected, analysed and made available to the business to enable better decision-making.

BENEFITS OF A CLEAR BRAND PURPOSE

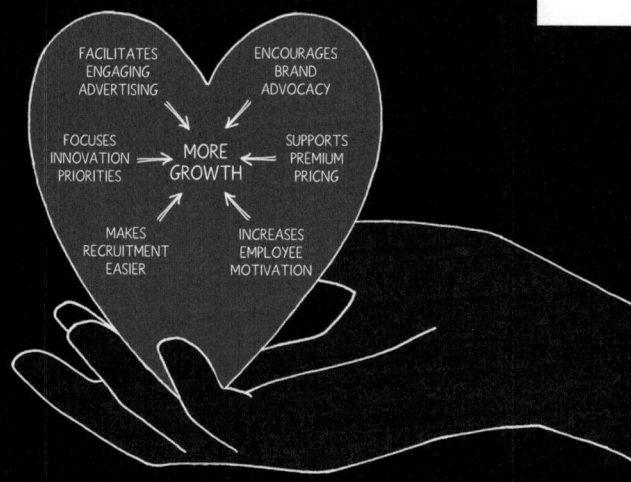

PART **TWO**

BRAND DEVELOPMENT

2.1 HOW BRANDS EXIST IN THE BRAIN

Brands are essentially memories: collections of connections in the brain, built up and constantly evolving over time as people have more experiences connected with the brand. The brand will be different from one individual to the next, depending on the set of experiences they have had.

A brand can be defined as the associations that spring to mind when people come across the brand. Associations can include the brand's name, its logo, what the product looks like and what it does. They can also include memories of using the brand, based on recent experience or long ago, and any words, sounds, images or ideas remembered from the brand's communications.

BRAND ASSOCIATIONS EXAMPLE

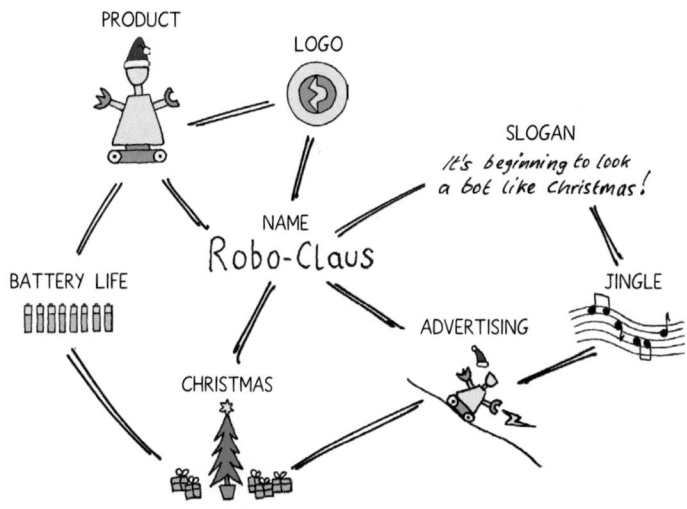

In this fictitious example, Robo-Claus is a toy robot for young children with interchangeable claws and a Santa's hat. It has been advertised for years as a must-have Christmas present. The ads feature stories of the robot using his versatile claws to help Santa deliver presents on Christmas Eve. Sadly, Robo-Claus is notorious for requiring a lot of battery power, which means he's usually out of action before Boxing Day. The diagram illustrates what Robo-Claus's dominant mental associations might look like.

A brand's associations influence whether it is bought or not, in the context of alternative choices and relative prices. They can affect purchasing immediately or decades later. Some ads that haven't been aired for over 50 years are still recalled vividly today;

a British ad featuring talking chimps taking a piano downstairs is a famous example. What matters to marketing is how all these associations shape purchase decisions, and how they could be developed so that more of the target audience is more predisposed to buy the brand in the future. The section that follows sets out a process that marketers can use to identify the associations best for growing the brand – the cornerstone of brand strategy.

2.2 BRAND PURPOSE AND STRATEGY

Brands are born when someone has an idea for a product that they believe others will want to buy. There's a reason for bringing the brand into the world – a clear purpose. Eric Ryan and Adam Lowry, cofounders of Method cleaning products, believed that people would pay more for eco-friendly products if they were both stylish and helped clean up the planet. The rapid growth of their brand proves they were right.

Business leaders need to be clear about what they want their brand to stand for because the commercial advantages of doing so are significant.

BENEFITS OF A CLEAR BRAND PURPOSE

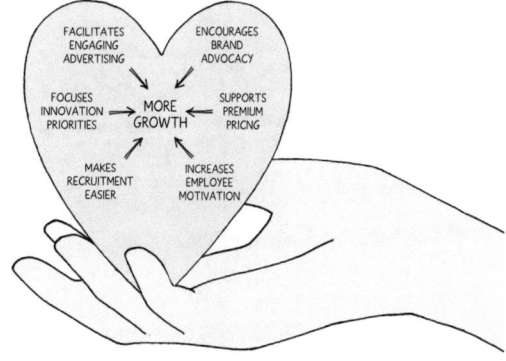

The brand purpose should be based on what the company does or could be best at, and on what the leaders and employees want it to be. A brand whose purpose stems from what the company already does but inspires employees to do it better, is more likely to succeed.

The 'value disciplines' framework, developed by business strategists Treacy and Wiersema in the 1990s, helps companies identify the area in which they have potential to rise above the competition and could use to define their brand purpose. The framework acknowledges that an organization operating in a competitive market with finite resources cannot be the best at everything.

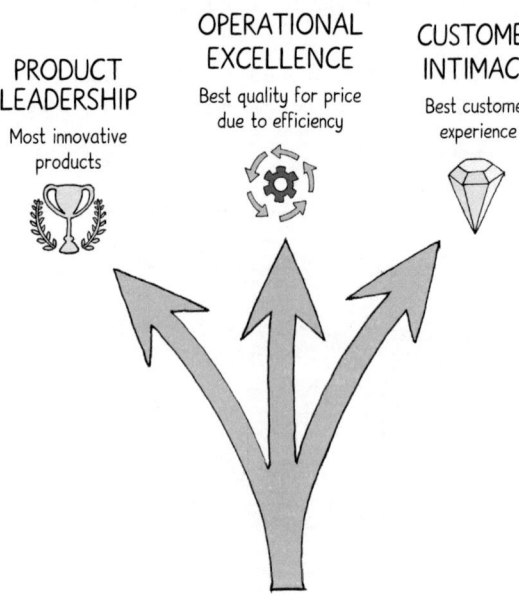

VALUE DISCIPLINES

PRODUCT LEADERSHIP
Most innovative products

OPERATIONAL EXCELLENCE
Best quality for price due to efficiency

CUSTOMER INTIMACY
Best customer experience

The framework highlights three potential disciplines in which to specialize, so that a customer who prizes one discipline in particular will value the brand above others. Successful companies deliver adequately in all disciplines but stand out from competitors in one. To do this, they focus their energy and resources on their chosen discipline rather than trying, and failing, to address every customer need.

The very best marketers either choose to work for a company with a clear brand purpose or inspire their company to discover (or rediscover) one. With a purpose in place that the company can rally behind, the next task is to develop the brand strategy. This is a business plan defining how the company will make money from products(s) using the brand name, which includes:

- A long-term financial objective (e.g., $400k annual profit within five years)
- A description of who will buy the brand based on the brand purpose (e.g., people with an annual income of greater than $75K who love driving but want to protect the planet)
- A definition of the product(s) that will be sold and when they will be launched and upgraded (e.g., expanded network of charging points in year two, a lighter model with double the battery capacity in year three)
- The numbers that will be sold each year and the average selling price (aligned with the financial objective)
- The associations that will be built around the brand to accelerate growth (captured in 'The Brand PIÑATA' described in the next section)

2.3 THE BRAND PIÑATA

The Brand PIÑATA (Proposition, Insight, Needs, Associations, Testaments and Assets) is a framework for defining what customers should associate with the brand so they are predisposed to buying it. Traditional frameworks such as the 'brand key' and the 'brand onion' encourage brand descriptions that are intellectually and linguistically complex, even though brands are stored in the brain in a much more simplistic, primal way. Brands exist as a collage of unprocessed fragments of sounds, images and ideas, connected with the brand in consumers' brains. These associations evoke feelings toward the brand that compete with those of competitors to determine which brand is chosen.

The Brand PIÑATA focuses attention on the elements that need to be established in consumers' minds in order to make the brand the most compelling choice.

BRAND PIÑATA

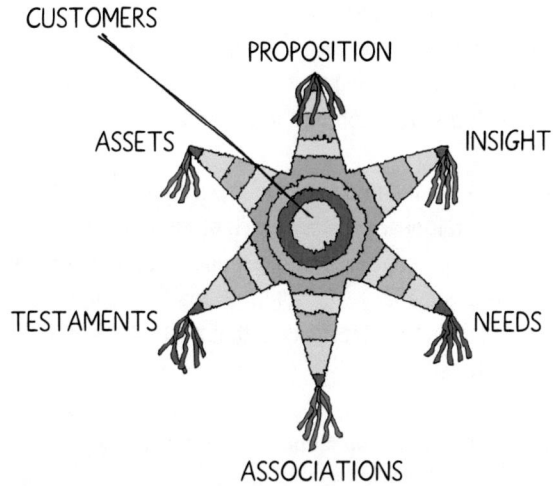

The customer definition and brand purpose are the starting point and should be signed off by the company's leaders because they affect all aspects of the business.

Next comes the insight. This is an idea connected to the brand's proposition that strongly resonates with the target audience. For the chocolate brand Snickers, the insight is people aren't themselves when they're hungry. We can all recognize this insight, and it relates to the brand's proposition: to fill people up when they're hungry.

The next step is to identify the needs and occasions when the brand should come to people's minds. The mental connection will be built by the brand's communications so that the brand springs to mind when someone realizes they have a need or desire for something. For example, when someone needs to buy lots of things for a new flat, IKEA might pop into their head.

The next step is to define the associations (ideas and feelings) and testaments (stories, claims, etc.) that should surface in the brain as soon as people think of the brand. If they're compelling enough, these connections will 'seal the deal,' making it easy for the customer to plan an IKEA trip without giving the decision a second thought.

Finally, to help the brand come easily and quickly to mind, it helps to have a set of 'distinctive assets' (visuals, sounds, words, customs, etc.) that are featured repeatedly across all the brand's touch-points. Twix's advertising of the 1980s was chock-full of sounds, images, phrases and jingles used to create a coherent, connected and longer-lasting set of memories surrounding the brand. More modern examples include M&S Food, Red Bull, Specsavers and, of course, Apple.

2.4 PRICE POSITIONING

The price of a brand is an integral part of its positioning. A brand designed to provide a superior experience and make customers feel proud to own it also needs a premium price. Louis Vuitton, Ferrari and Apple always maintain their prices because they know that discounting can seriously undermine a premium brand's appeal. Conversely, a brand designed to attract customers through low prices should avoid upmarket packaging that would confuse how people think of the brand. Price needs to be aligned with the rest of the mix.

ALIGNING THE MARKETING MIX AROUND PRICE POINT

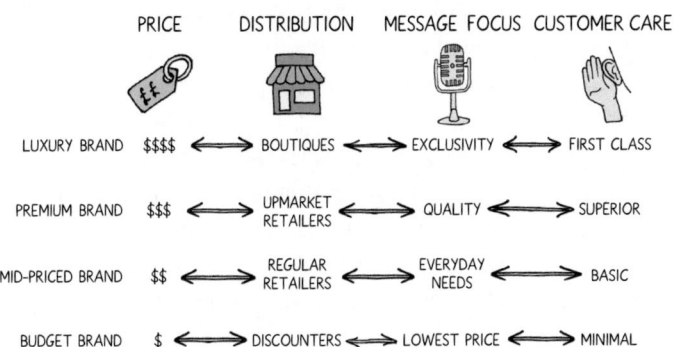

	PRICE	DISTRIBUTION	MESSAGE FOCUS	CUSTOMER CARE
LUXURY BRAND	$$$$	BOUTIQUES	EXCLUSIVITY	FIRST CLASS
PREMIUM BRAND	$$$	UPMARKET RETAILERS	QUALITY	SUPERIOR
MID-PRICED BRAND	$$	REGULAR RETAILERS	EVERYDAY NEEDS	BASIC
BUDGET BRAND	$	DISCOUNTERS	LOWEST PRICE	MINIMAL

Once the prices of brands in a market have been broadly established, the room for manoeuvre is limited. A premium brand cannot drop its price much before becoming unprofitable, and a budget brand would not have the credibly to increase its price significantly unless it had been completely repositioned, which is slow and expensive. Consumers use price as one the indicators of a brand's quality and worth, and if they do compare prices, they tend to do so among brands within the same price bracket. BMW's prices are compared with Audi, while Ford's prices are compared with Peugeot, etc. Most people choose between a small 'consideration set' of brands that meet their needs closely enough and compare their prices. Someone might prefer a particular brand but will be happy to choose an alternative if the price difference is large enough, so even a strong brand's price can't stray too far from its peers.

There is, however, a way to command a high price and not be tethered to other brands, and that is to be seen as something different. If consumers don't directly see a brand as similar to others, they won't compare prices. And since people don't make absolute judgments about how much a brand is worth, a unique brand can charge a high price. Take Nespresso as an example. When Nespresso was launched, people saw it as something completely new and different, not comparable to instant coffee, which is why the brand was able to charge 30 cents a cup instead of five. If people did compare the price of Nespresso with anything, it was with the three dollars or so they were used to paying for similar drinks in coffee shops. This tendency for people to judge value in relation to other things and not in an absolute way is known in psychology as 'anchoring.' When launching a premium-priced product, people should be encouraged to compare it with a much more expensive 'anchor.'

2.5 BRAND KPIs

Businesses often use key performance indicators (KPIs) to track their progress and identify areas requiring greater management focus and support. Leadership teams refer to KPI reports to adjust company activities and maximize the chances of targets being achieved. Dashboards visualizing the KPIs can indicate where the business is on or ahead of target by colouring the corresponding KPI green. Where performance is close to target, it can be coloured grey; where it is significantly behind target, it can be coloured red. Looking at the KPIs in this way reveals, at a glance, the overall business performance and any areas to be celebrated or prioritized for extra attention.

In the long run, the most relevant indicators of business success are, of course, financial. As far as owners/shareholders are concerned, profit is usually paramount. Reporting business KPIs in a pyramid format allows profit to sit at the top. It also illustrates how all aspects of the company's delivery, represented by the metrics lower in the pyramid, contribute to the ultimate financial objective.

BUSINESS KPI PYRAMID

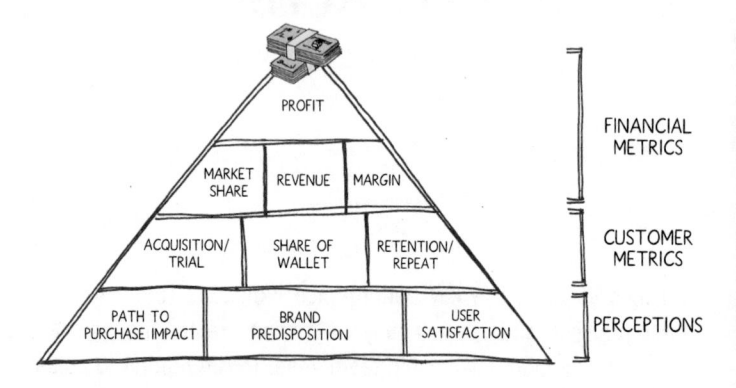

```
                    PROFIT
          ┌──────────┬─────────┬────────┐
          │  MARKET  │ REVENUE │ MARGIN │
          │  SHARE   │         │        │
       ┌──┴──────┬───┴─────┬───┴────────┴──┐
       │ACQUISI- │ SHARE OF│ RETENTION/   │
       │TION/    │ WALLET  │ REPEAT       │
       │TRIAL    │         │              │
    ┌──┴─────────┼─────────┼──────────────┴──┐
    │ PATH TO    │  BRAND  │      USER       │
    │ PURCHASE   │ PREDIS- │  SATISFACTION   │
    │ IMPACT     │POSITION │                 │
    └────────────┴─────────┴─────────────────┘
```

- FINANCIAL METRICS
- CUSTOMER METRICS
- PERCEPTIONS

A cleverly organized pyramid highlights how profit performance can be understood by looking at changes in market share, revenue and margin. Likewise, market share performance can be understood by looking at changes in customer metrics such as acquisition or trial, share of wallet and retention or repeat.

In order for the role of marketing to be appreciated within a business and for its impact on these metrics to be recognized, the company's KPIs should also include metrics related to the 'perceptions' marketing shapes in order to influence the customer metrics.

Some good options for brand KPIs include:

BRAND PREDISPOSITION
– Measured among the whole target audience
- Percentage that have heard of the brand's name
- Percentage saying they'd consider the brand
- Level of Google searches featuring the brand

PATH TO PURCHASE IMPACT
– Measured among people who have bought the category recently
- Percentage noticing the brand in the run-up to their purchase (in search results, on websites, in stores, etc.) and more positive toward brand afterwards
- Percentage talking to a salesperson and more positive toward the brand afterwards
- Price quoted/seen compared to other brands

USER SATISFACTION
– Measured among customers
- Net promoter score (NPS) (the percent giving a brand score of 9 or 10 score on a 'likelihood to recommend' scale minus the percent giving a score of 6 or below)
- Average user review scores
- Percentage experiencing problems or making complaints
- Percentage experiencing problems or making complaints that were not resolved

PART **THREE**

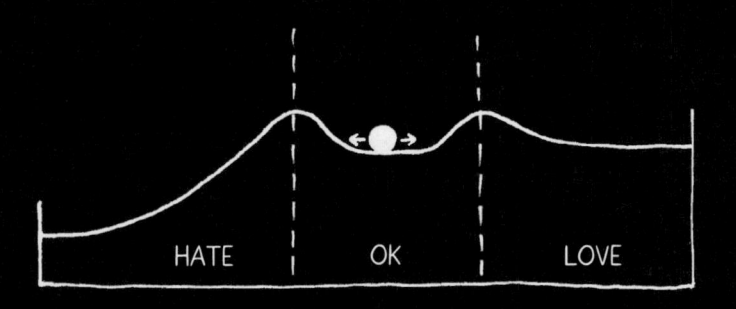

HATE | OK | LOVE

BRAND EXPERIENCE

3.1 DEFINING THE BRAND EXPERIENCE

People's perceptions of a brand are shaped to some extent by every experience connected with the brand. Brands need to manage all possible touchpoints, particularly in luxury categories in which customers expect more and are less forgiving if standards slip. Optimal delivery requires careful curation of the whole customer journey, every aspect of an encounter and for the five senses to be catered to.

THE WHOLE JOURNEY

Since any encounter could strengthen or damage brand perceptions, marketers should consider what people experience when they are exploring a purchase, when making a purchase and once they are customers.

When buying a new car, for example, customers will already have an impression of the brand from its advertising and website. How the cars are presented at the showroom, interactions with sales representatives, the feeling of sitting inside the car and how it drives will all shape customer opinions, as will the process of selecting features, negotiating the price and organizing payment. After the sale, follow-up communications and the manner in which problems are handled will continue to influence the brand relationship.

EVERY ASPECT OF AN ENCOUNTER

Customer-centric companies review brand encounters from many angles, looking for any opportunities to make them more positive.

FOUR ASPECTS OF BRAND ENCOUNTERS

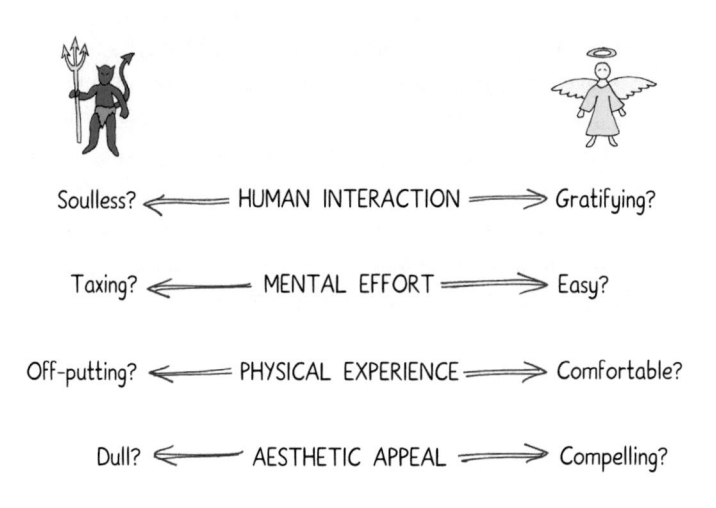

Soulless? ⟵ HUMAN INTERACTION ⟶ Gratifying?

Taxing? ⟵ MENTAL EFFORT ⟶ Easy?

Off-putting? ⟵ PHYSICAL EXPERIENCE ⟶ Comfortable?

Dull? ⟵ AESTHETIC APPEAL ⟶ Compelling?

Starbucks creates an agreeable in-store experience by training its staff via Starbucks Experience classes, making the shops welcoming and comfortable and enabling customers to order and pay for their favourite drink in seconds.

CATERING TO THE FIVE SENSES

Most brands pay attention to the visual side of their presentation, but experiences can be enhanced greatly if they appeal to multiple senses. Retailers, airlines and car manufacturers have long been managing the aromas and sounds associated with their brands. Victoria's Secret, for example, plays classical music in store to create an air of sophistication. Car manufacturer Mitsubishi even managed to replicate its leathery new car smell in special newspaper ads, which resulted in the model featured selling out within two weeks. The power of touch was well demonstrated when UK supermarket Asda created packaging allowing customer to feel the texture of its own label toilet paper and needed to double its shelf space to reflect the increased demand. Triggering multiple senses can make an experience more positive and memorable and help reinforce what sets the brand apart from others.

3.2 IDENTIFYING THE MOMENTS THAT MATTER

Most day-to-day interactions only have a small impact on brand perceptions but there are occasional, critical moments that can make or break the relationship depending on what customers experience. If customer relationships typically oscillate within a zone of indifference, critical moments may push people into either a close relationship that's easy to maintain or a strained relationship that is hard to recover from.

THE TOPOGRAPHY OF CUSTOMER RELATIONSHIPS

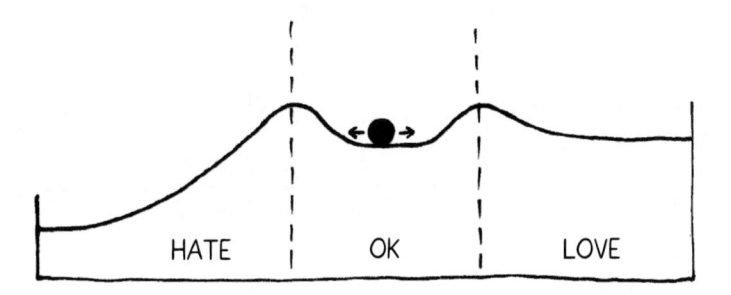

HATE OK LOVE

The next step is to establish, using market research, the moments that matter most. Where are the pain points? What annoys people when things don't work well and delights them when they do? Brands can achieve a better return on investment if they focus on ways to make miserable moments less likely and magical moments more frequent rather than becoming more efficient in less-important areas.

To identify the moments that matter, the first step is to map the entire customer journey, covering the touchpoints people use when researching a purchase, making a purchase and all the occasions and ways they contact the brand as a customer. Marketers can use the grid below to help identify customer interaction priorities. It shows five common types of interaction with spaces for entering an assessment of how well the brand performs.

CUSTOMER INTERACTION PERFORMANCE GRID

	Easy to find out how?	Completed quickly?	Satisfactory outcomes?	Agreeable experience?
INFORMATION				
ENQUIRIES				
PURCHASING				
USER SUPPORT				
COMPLAINTS				

The grid is most helpful if the marketer has a good understanding of what makes customers tick, what they're looking for and what frustrates them. For maximum benefit, brands should focus on improving in areas of the grid where the brand is currently weak and which customers care about most.

3.3 CUSTOMER SERVICE EXCELLENCE

In some categories, a major component of the brand experience comes from human interaction, such as at premium hotels, restaurants and retailers, to name a few. Brands in these categories need their client-facing employees to be emotionally intelligent, attuned to customers' needs, knowledgeable about the brand's offer and motivated to look after customers. Having committed employees kick-starts a chain of benefits.

EMPLOYEE COMMITMENT VIRTUOUS CIRCLE

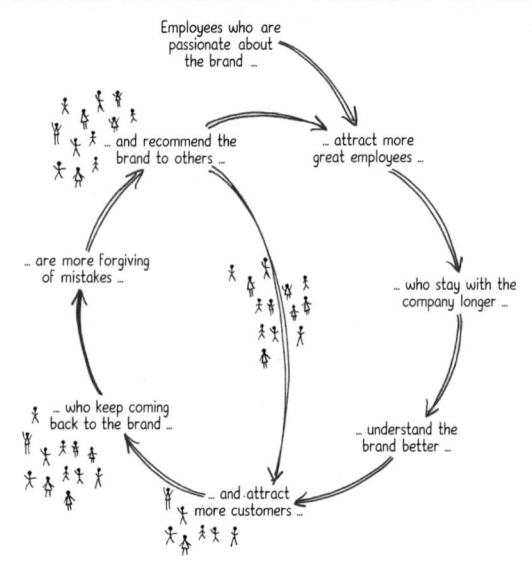

Employees who are passionate about the brand ...

... attract more great employees ...

... who stay with the company longer ...

... understand the brand better ...

... and attract more customers ...

... who keep coming back to the brand ...

... are more forgiving of mistakes ...

... and recommend the brand to others ...

The cycle starts with careful employee selection. If client service is crucial, client-facing vacancies should be filled by applicants who show not only the right skills but also a belief in the brand and its purpose. The benefits of high employee engagement are well documented – they are more loyal and more productive, boosting customer acquisition, satisfaction and retention.

Online shoe and clothing retailer Zappos is famous for the loyalty of its staff and quality of its customer service. To ensure all its employees truly believe in the brand, job applicants are thoroughly screened so that their values match those of Zappos. Additionally, new employees' commitment is tested by offering them $2,000 to quit after two weeks of training if they're not convinced that they fit the company's culture.

Big companies can be seen as greedy and impersonal, so brands that genuinely care about their customers are greatly appreciated. US grocery chain Trader Joe's is a brand that puts people first and gives employees the freedom to support customers as they see fit. In one of many examples, an 89-year-old man was housebound during a snowstorm and his granddaughter called several grocery stores asking if they would deliver to make sure he had sufficient supplies to last through the cold spell. She had no luck until Trader Joe's said they would help, even though they don't normally deliver. They arrived within 30 minutes and, as a gesture of goodwill, decided not to charge the old man. The company did not try to publicize the good deed, but it went viral anyway when the granddaughter tweeted about it.

Once recruited, people are more likely to stay with a company and promote it effectively if they are treated well and can see the brand is true to its word. Microsoft has repeatedly been ranked as one of the best companies to work for in the US because of how it advances equal pay across genders, offers salaries that match or exceed the cost of living, provides workers with a generous benefits package and reduces waste and energy usage.

In a world where consumers understand and appreciate the value of equality and conservation better than previously, companies that strive to do the right thing are increasingly attractive to both workers and customers.

3.4 HANDLING COMPLAINTS

How complaints are handled has a major impact on customer relationships. A customer who is pleased by how their issue was handled may become a brand advocate, whereas a disgruntled customer is likely to discredit the brand at every opportunity. When an issue occurs, it should be easy for the customer to find out how to flag it, ideally choosing their favourite channel such as email, telephone or online chat. From then on, there is a proven formula for ensuring the matter is handled well.

HANDLING CUSTOMER COMPLAINTS

RESPOND QUICKLY ⇒ APOLOGIZE & THANK ⇒ LISTEN & UNDERSTAND ⇒ ASK DESIRED OUTCOME ⇒ SUGGEST SOLUTION(S)

RESPOND QUICKLY

The quicker a complaint can be addressed, the better. A drawn-out process frustrates customers and makes them less likely to accept proposed solutions. As a rule of thumb, it should be no more than one to two days between the initial contact and a solution being offered. Many companies scour social media posts for customers expressing dissatisfaction with their service and try to resolve the problem quickly to prevent any further negative word of mouth and to show how responsive the company is.

APOLOGIZE AND THANK

Acknowledging that the problem has inconvenienced or annoyed the customer is an important step that helps establish rapport, without needing to admit responsibility for what has happened. Thanking the customer for giving the company an opportunity to put things right is also a great way to foster a constructive atmosphere. After all, many customers choose to express their displeasure by simply moving their business elsewhere.

LISTEN AND UNDERSTAND

As with any conflict, a customer complaint can usually be diffused by asking the customer to explain the situation and listening to them properly, probing for clarification and playing back what they've said. Customer service teams should be trained in how to interact with customers and never be given a script to follow, time limits or quotas.

ASK DESIRED OUTCOME
Once they've aired their complaint, the next step is to ask them what an acceptable solution would be. If their request falls within guidelines, it should be met. Quite often, however, the customer isn't sure what they want and is expecting a suggestion.

SUGGEST SOLUTION(S)
Suggested solutions should reflect the details of the issue and reflect the level of inconvenience to the customer and degree to which the company is responsible. The customer service team needs flexibility in the solutions it can offer and to use judgment as to what is fair and appropriate without additional levels of approval if these would cause delay.

In addition to adopting this best-practice approach, customer service teams should avoid the following:

- Passing the customer from one person to another
- Questioning the customer's accuracy or honesty
- Explaining what the customer did wrong
- Making excuses or blaming partner businesses (e.g., delivery companies)

3.5 CUSTOMER MANAGEMENT SYSTEMS

Companies need a systematic way to ensure high standards of customer service are being maintained and to flag problems in time for remedial action to be taken.

ADDRESSING BRAND DELIVERY PROBLEMS IN REAL TIME

CUSTOMER EXPERIENCES A PROBLEM

⇓

HAS OPPORTUNITY TO FLAG PROBLEM

⇓

ALERT SENT TO EMPLOYEES ABLE TO ADDRESS PROBLEM

↙ ↘

CUSTOMER CONTACTED TO MAKE AMENDS

ACTIONS TAKEN TO ELIMINATE PROBLEM

ALLOWING CUSTOMERS TO FLAG A PROBLEM

The best way to do this depends on the type of interaction but the priority is to make it quick and easy. Customer help areas or QR codes in stores, SMS, email, apps or social media channels are all suitable mechanisms. In face-to-face situations, simply checking that customers are satisfied is good practice.

ALERTING RELEVANT EMPLOYEES

Regardless of how an issue has been highlighted, it needs to be directed to whomever is in a position to address it. This could be as simple as a well-ingrained protocol or as sophisticated as a 'closed-loop' customer experience management system. What's important is that the information is relayed and can be acted upon quickly.

SUPPORTING THE AFFECTED CUSTOMER

The customer who identified the problem should be handled according to normal procedures (see Section 3.4). If the customer mentioned the problem just to be helpful, offering them a small reward (e.g., a money-off voucher) is a nice gesture.

ELIMINATING THE PROBLEM

If the problem could affect other customers, action should be taken to solve the problem and avoid further customers being inconvenienced or disappointed.

PART FOUR

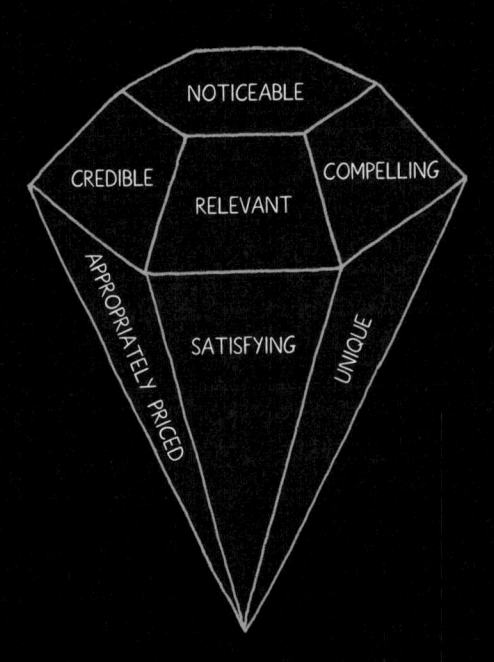

INNOVATION

4.1 INNOVATION STRATEGY

Innovation is an area that many businesses struggle with. The *Harvard Business Review* reported in 2016 that 94% of global executives were dissatisfied with their organization's innovation performance. These leaders know that innovation success has a huge influence on a company's long-term commercial viability. Given the cost of product development and the fact that the majority of new products fail (70% of consumer-packaged goods, for example), even a modest improvement in the odds of success provides a major competitive advantage. Companies that innovate well and use the profits to fund further innovation make it hard for competitors to keep up.

The chances of success can be enhanced by:

- Identifying the approach to innovation best suited to the company
- Being clear on what innovation needs to achieve
- Coming up with strong ideas and using consumer feedback to guide development

There are three broad approaches to innovation a business can take.

DIFFERENT APPROACHES TO INNOVATION

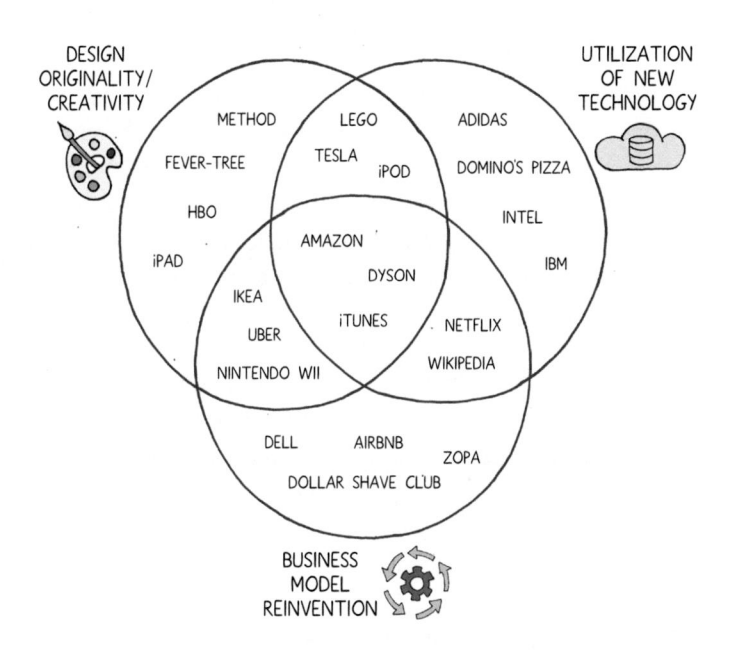

DESIGN ORIGINALITY/ CREATIVITY

UTILIZATION OF NEW TECHNOLOGY

BUSINESS MODEL REINVENTION

- METHOD
- FEVER-TREE
- HBO
- iPAD
- LEGO
- TESLA
- iPOD
- ADIDAS
- DOMINO'S PIZZA
- INTEL
- IBM
- AMAZON
- DYSON
- IKEA
- iTUNES
- UBER
- NINTENDO WII
- NETFLIX
- WIKIPEDIA
- DELL
- AIRBNB
- ZOPA
- DOLLAR SHAVE CLUB

Which approach or combination of approaches a business should take depends on its strengths versus competitors and how likely the industry is to be disrupted by new business models.

Kodak engineer Steve Sasson invented the digital camera in 1975. According to Sasson, the reaction from company management was that the concept was ingenious but that he shouldn't tell anyone about it. Kodak saw itself as a manufacturer of photographic film, paper and chemicals and treated digital photography as an enemy to be defeated. If it had, instead, seen itself as a company helping people capture and share memories, it might have avoided bankruptcy.

If disruption is on its way, marketers need to seize the opportunity, and if that means reshaping an established business, so be it.

Even if technology won't bring about new business models, every brand should look for opportunities to use technology to enhance consumer value before competitors do. According to Dennis Maloney, Chief Digital Officer at Domino's Pizza, the company went from being a pizza company that sells online to an e-commerce company that sells pizza and became the world's largest pizza chain as a result.

Technology isn't essential to great innovation. Creative ideas can be just as, if not more, important. Companies such as Nintendo, HBO, Pixar and Lego thrive thanks to a continual flow of original and imaginative ideas that surprise and delight their customers. When Sony and Microsoft launched consoles with state-of-the-art technology, Nintendo managed to attract a whole new demographic to the category with the Wii, a low-specification console with totally new types of game and fitness activities.

4.2 INNOVATION PROCESS

Once the overall approach has been defined, marketers can turn their attention to the innovation brief. People buy products to make their lives better, so an innovation brief starts with defining the aspect of the consumer's life the innovation should aim to enhance. If the brand has a clearly defined purpose, the brief is straightforward, since all innovation should be designed to enable the brand to fulfil its purpose better.

The innovation process initiated by the brief follows three phases: idea generation, development of the most promising ideas and full production of any that the business is confident will succeed. The moments when decisions are made about which ideas to continue with are often referred to as 'gates.'

INNOVATION DEVELOPMENT PROCESS

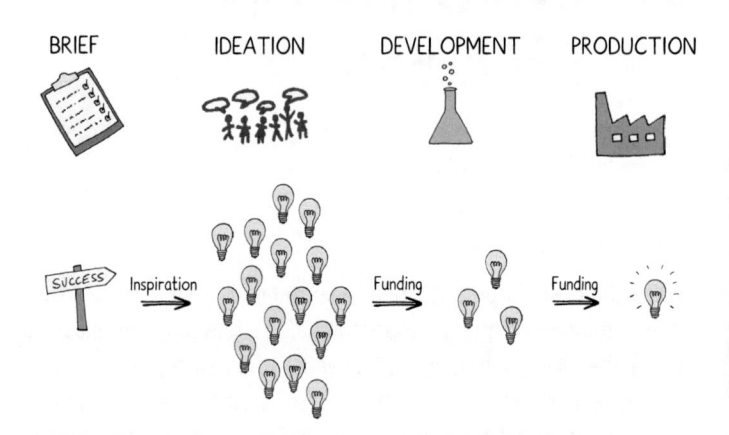

Many industries have adopted 'agile' principles in their innovation processes. This involves developing prototypes as early as possible and obtaining consumer feedback to guide further iterations or to shelve the idea if the feedback isn't sufficiently promising.

Agile innovation has many advantages over the traditional, linear approach, especially for markets where consumer priorities or new technologies change quickly, and products need to be refreshed frequently in order to keep up.

TRADITIONAL VS AGILE DEVELOPMENT

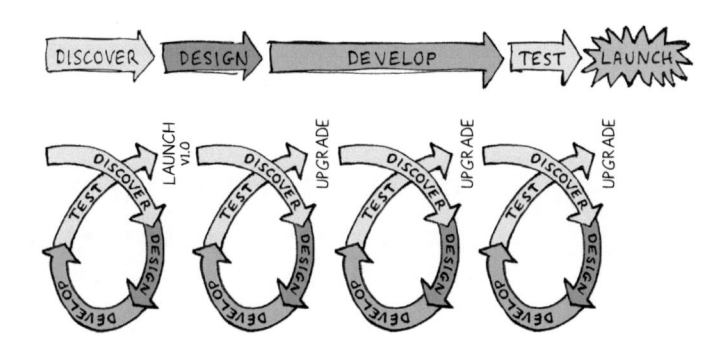

With the traditional approach, the full product design is finalized early on, and there is a lengthy development phase during which all the product features are built. Problems arise if final testing reveals that the product designed possibly a year or so previously is no longer quite what consumers want. Time and money may have been wasted on features that are now irrelevant and other more important features may be missing.

The main benefits of the agile approach are that it yields a basic prototype quickly and at low cost and that development can be focused on whichever new features will add most value to the next iteration, even if priorities evolve over time. Products are, in effect, always a work in progress, shaped by the people who pay for them.

For agile development to work well, marketing, R&D, production, sales and market research teams all need to work collaboratively to shape ideas and determine how products can be developed, produced and upgraded, making best use of the company's resources.

4.3 GENERATING INNOVATION IDEAS

It's good practice to set aside time, once or twice a year, to generate ideas for enhancing customer value and reviewing innovation priorities.

GENERATING GREAT INNOVATION IDEAS

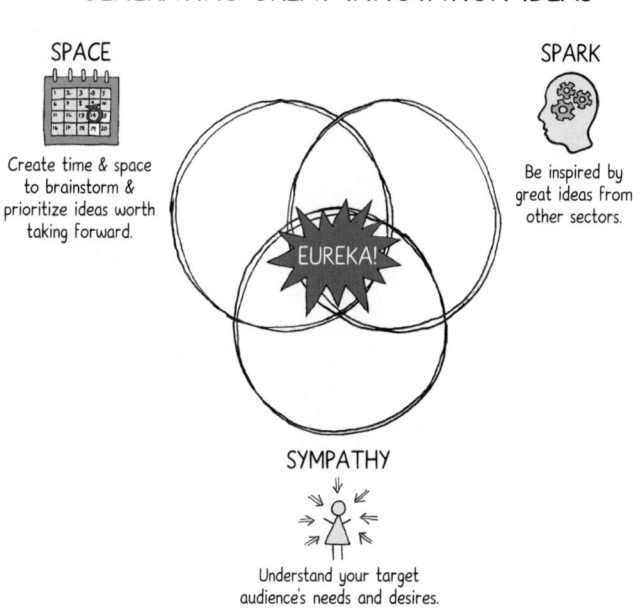

SPACE

Create time & space to brainstorm & prioritize ideas worth taking forward.

SPARK

Be inspired by great ideas from other sectors.

EUREKA!

SYMPATHY

Understand your target audience's needs and desires.

SPACE
For an 'ideation' session to be effective, attendees need be in an environment that encourages creativity. Natural light, bright colours, space to move around, fresh air and an inclusive, trusting atmosphere can all make a huge difference to the quantity and quality of ideas generated.

SYMPATHY
The most powerful ideas come from a deep understanding of the consumer, so the team should be immersed in information and insights about the target audience, including their needs and desires related to the category and beyond.

SPARK
Creativity occurs when two separate ideas are brought together to produce something new. Exposing people to innovation in other fields and sectors is a good way to spark ideas, particularly if this includes examples of how new technologies have been used to enhance products and customer experiences.

A good way of providing inspiration is to use an ideas springboard matrix. The marketing/market research team needs to spend time discovering the latest thinking and innovation in areas that could spark relevant ideas for the brand. The fields listed in the matrix below are a useful starting point. In the ideation session, the team hears about the latest developments in these areas and explores whether a similar idea might create customer value in the brand's category.

IDEAS SPRINGBOARD MATRIX

WHAT'S HAPPENING IN ...

	VISUAL ARTS	ERGONOMICS	PORTABLE TECH	APPS	E-PAYMENT	INTERNET OF THINGS	MACHINE LEARNING	ROBOTICS	FAST FOOD (E.G.)	JAPAN (E.G.)
PRODUCTS										
FUTURE PRODUCTS										
CUSTOMER EXPERIENCE										
DISTRIBUTION										
SALES										
MARKETING										
PRICING STRATEGY										
OWNED MEDIA										
SOCIAL MEDIA										
CUSTOMER HELPLINE										

THAT WE COULD LEVERAGE IN OUR ...

The matrix highlights the variety of ways in which a brand could innovate to serve customers better. The most successful brands consider how every element of the marketing mix could contribute to a better brand experience, from the communications and sales experience to after-sales and beyond, drawing on the latest ideas, wherever they come from.

4.4 ASSESSING INNOVATION POTENTIAL

Companies that generate lots of great innovation ideas are likely to be the most successful, but only if they know how to identify the ones with true potential.

Ideas to develop, and ultimately launch, should be selected using a set of proven success criteria such as 'the seven facets of an innovation gem': noticeable, relevant, credible, compelling, appropriately priced, satisfying and unique.

THE SEVEN FACETS OF AN INNOVATION GEM

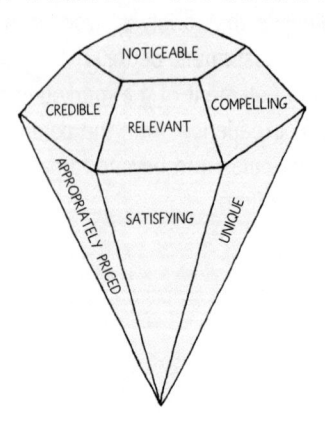

NOTICEABLE
New products benefit from having a way to stand out from the crowd. Distinctive names, logos and packaging can all help.

RELEVANT
Whatever the product is or does, consumers must be able to see its value to them.

CREDIBLE
People must believe that the product is likely to deliver on its promise. Brands with a reliable track record have an advantage here.

COMPELLING
In many categories, consumers have a number of relevant alternatives available to them, so the product needs to be highly compelling if it is to be chosen above others. This is especially true if buying the product requires significant effort from the customer, such as switching bank accounts.

APPROPRIATELY PRICED
The price needs to be in line with whatever consumers consider to be comparable alternatives. The goal is a for a win-win situation: consumers feel they are getting good value when paying the asking price and the business makes a good profit.

SATISFYING
The long-term success of a product depends mainly on how well it lives up to expectations. If customers are highly satisfied with their experience, not only are they likely to continue buying it, but they're also more likely to recommend it and to buy other products from the brand.

UNIQUE

In any competitive market, brands are constantly vying for consumers' attention, so even a product with a lot to offer can be lost in the noise and fade from memory quickly. Having a unique, distinctive characteristic helps a product stick in mind. If the characteristic also reminds people of the brand's benefits, it can encourage a trial and give users a justification for continuing to buy the brand. When Toilet Duck launched in the early 1980s, it was essentially the same as existing brands of toilet cleaner, but the bottle had a unique feature – a neck shaped like that of a duck that made it easier to squirt the liquid under the toilet rim. This feature helped the brand quickly become a market leader, command a higher price than any competitor for more than ten years, and ensure high brand saliency to this day.

4.5 LAUNCHING NEW PRODUCTS

The launch phase of a new product usually determines its fate. It is rare to be given a second chance if the product fails the first time around, so product launches need to be planned with care.

A successful launch involves six overlapping steps.

SIX STEPS TO LAUNCH SUCCESS

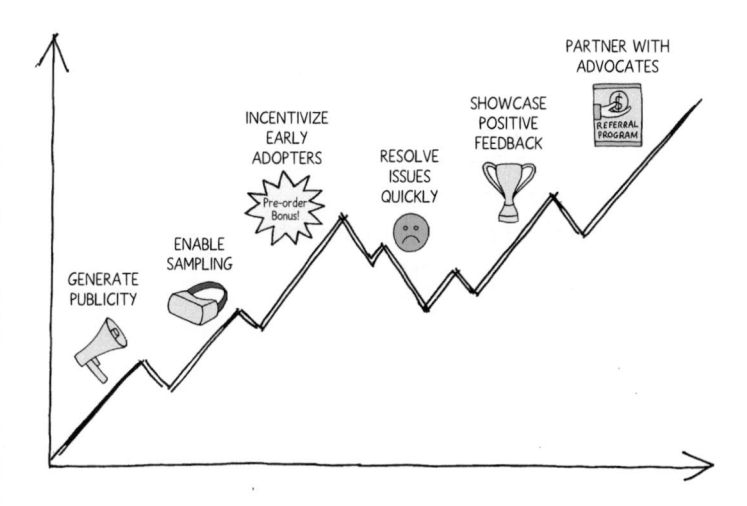

- GENERATE PUBLICITY
- ENABLE SAMPLING
- INCENTIVIZE EARLY ADOPTERS
- RESOLVE ISSUES QUICKLY
- SHOWCASE POSITIVE FEEDBACK
- PARTNER WITH ADVOCATES

GENERATE PUBLICITY

There is a limited window for creating publicity by virtue of the product being new, so this should be seized upon. In categories such as movies and video games, the window starts when the product is announced and peaks just before release; in other categories, it spans just a few weeks following the launch. Used at the right time, launch publicity encourages potential customers to seek out more information about the product and be more likely to consider it.

ENABLE SAMPLING

Sampling is highly effective for any product with a great user experience. In Tesla showrooms, people sit in the stylish, high-tech cars and imagine owning one. Test drives provide a taste of the unique and enjoyable driving experience. Letting people 'have' something for a while makes them like it more – an effect known as endowment. It also makes them want to buy it afterwards. This is known as loss aversion. Great products should be put into the hands of as many people as possible.

INCENTIVIZE EARLY ADOPTERS

Incentivizing early adopters is important because they tend to express their opinions about new products in social media and reviews. Assuming the product is good, this will encourage more buyers. Incentives can include lower pricing or bonus content available for a limited period after launch.

RESOLVE ISSUES QUICKLY
Most product launches experience teething problems, but these shouldn't derail a launch provided they are detected and resolved quickly. In this age of social media, brushing problems under the carpet or not providing fair compensation is foolhardier than ever.

SHOWCASE POSITIVE FEEDBACK
The product testimonial, in which fans of a product talk about its virtues, is a reliable form of advertising and especially valuable if potential customers are sceptical about claims being made about the product. For decades, Dove grew its market share by using testimonials to showcase the benefits of a soap containing moisturizers. It pays to make it easy for fans to express their positive impressions and share these widely in order to attract more buyers.

PARTNER WITH ADVOCATES
'Herd behaviour' is the tendency for people to follow what other people are doing rather than make up their own minds. This phenomenon explains why people gravitate toward products they think are popular and are used by celebrities, bloggers and vloggers. Teaming up with these influencers can therefore be a highly effective way to promote a new product.

PART **FIVE**

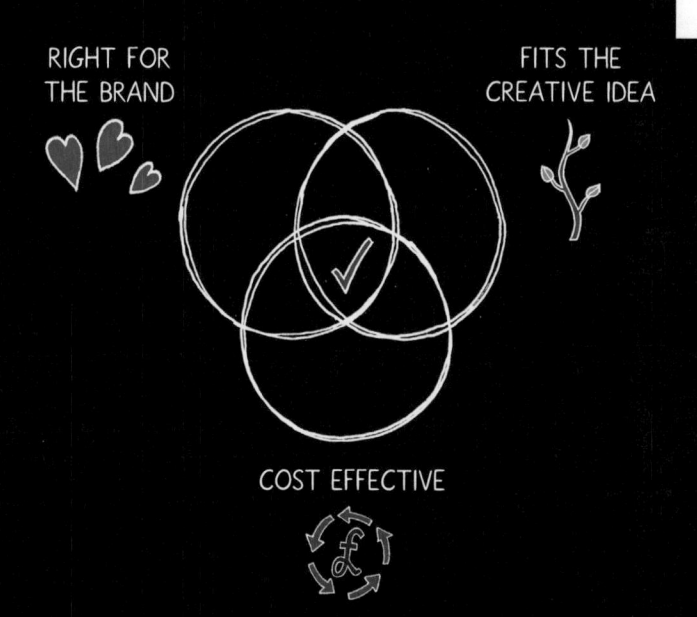

RIGHT FOR THE BRAND

FITS THE CREATIVE IDEA

COST EFFECTIVE

COMMUNICATIONS

5.1 HOW COMMUNICATIONS WORK

Communications are any experiences affecting the brand's mental associations apart from the experience of using the product. Paid, owned and earned media are the main communication channels (see Section 1.4). Where, when and how people are exposed to communications varies by channel but the psychological processes that influence brand choice are the same.

HOW COMMUNICATIONS INFLUENCE BRAND CHOICE

COMMAND ATTENTION

FORGE BRAND ASSOCIATIONS

INFLUENCE DECISIONS

ENHANCE USER SATISFACTION

COMMAND ATTENTION

To have any effect, communications need to command people's attention. Paid and owned media grab attention if they're different enough from their environment to stand out and hold attention and if they're perceived to be personally relevant or trigger an emotional reaction. People pay attention to earned media if they have an interest in the category or come across it while researching a purchase, provided the source is credible.

FORGE BRAND ASSOCIATIONS

If people pay attention to a piece of communication, they remember the most memorable aspects of what they see and hear. If these include the brand, the communications will forge new brand associations or strengthen existing ones. For communications to be effective, these associations need to be relevant to purchase decisions and, ideally, conjure positive feelings toward the brand.

INFLUENCE DECISIONS

Associations created by communications pop into people's brains when they come across the brand or when the brand comes to mind, making it feel like the right choice. The effect can be immediate, for example if someone searches for the category, notices one of the ads, clicks on it and makes a purchase. Potentially, the effect could last for decades; advertising seen in childhood can make people receptive toward a brand for the rest of their lives. The impact lasts for as long as the associations formed by the advertising remain in memory and continue to be relevant.

ENHANCE USER SATISFACTION

Communications can also enhance how people feel about the brand when they're using it, by showcasing what it excels at. Food retailer Marks & Spencer is famous for mouth-watering advertising that emphasizes the quality of its food and evokes the pleasure of eating it. This makes users more likely to notice and appreciate the quality of the food and feel that the brand is worth buying again.

5.2 USING COMMUNICATIONS TO BUILD A BRAND

Most brands could benefit from communications at some stage but the return on investment depends on the strength of what the brand has to offer. Stronger brands achieve greater returns because customers attracted by the communications are likely to remain loyal and provide significant long-term profit. Conversely, even brilliant communications cannot compensate for a substandard product because repeat purchase levels and word of mouth will ultimately determine the brand's fate.

The role communications can play depends on the brand's life stage.

ROLE OF COMMUNICATIONS AT DIFFERENT BRAND LIFE STAGES

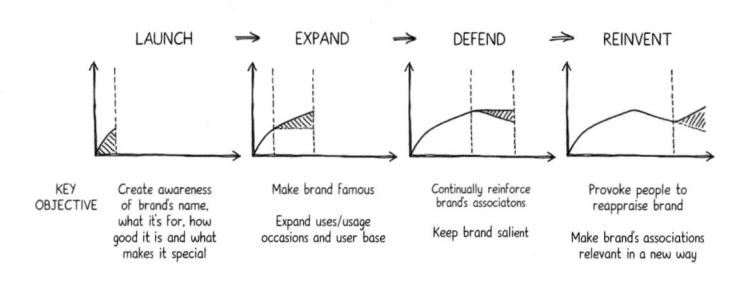

LAUNCH → EXPAND → DEFEND → REINVENT

KEY OBJECTIVE			
Create awareness of brand's name, what it's for, how good it is and what makes it special	Make brand famous Expand uses/usage occasions and user base	Continually reinforce brand's associatons Keep brand salient	Provoke people to reappraise brand Make brand's associations relevant in a new way

LAUNCH
Early on, communications can accelerate growth by raising awareness of the brand, what's special about it and how this benefits the buyer. Doing this quickly is important, as competitors are likely to launch copycat 'me too' products. To capitalize on 'first mover advantage,' a brand needs to be well established before alternatives are available.

The launch phase should continue until most of the brand's potential customers know what it offers. The old adage that people need to hear a marketing message at least seven times before acting upon it illustrates the value of repetition. Multiple exposures help a brand's message to sink in and even make people like and trust the brand more because of what's known as the 'mere exposure effect.'

EXPAND
After the launch phase, the brand should focus on becoming famous, so people automatically think of it when then they have a need or desire the brand could fufil. This allows the brand to make money from new users and usage occasions. Retail giant Amazon spent three years establishing itself as a fast, good value, trustworthy online retailer selling books before capitalizing on this reputation to sell CDs, electronics, toys and other goods.

DEFEND

Once a brand is well known, it can continue to be profitable so long as its proposition remains relevant, and competitors fail to encroach on its territory. For 100 years, Volvo has emphasized the safety and durability of its cars, which means that the brand comes to mind when people think about buying a family car. Volvo has protected this market position by continually developing and advertising new technologies that improve safety levels.

REINVENT

Long-established brands decline if they are associated with needs or desires that are becoming less relevant or because they are no longer salient in category buyers' minds. Provided the products themselves are strong, communications might be able to reverse the brand's fortunes. In 2010, men's grooming brand Old Spice repositioned itself with 'The Man Your Man Could Smell Like' campaign. The advertising, and the earned media it provoked, brought an old-fashioned brand to the attention of a whole new generation. While rare, brand reinventions like this are possible if the communications are highly creative, original and resonate powerfully with the target audience.

5.3 CHOOSING THE RIGHT TYPES OF MEDIA

The types of media a brand should use depends on the role of communications within the growth strategy. The first decision is how paid, owned and earned media should be utilized.

In some categories, paid media are essential because they are as much a part of the brand experience as the products themselves. Fine fragrance brands, for example, cannot differentiate themselves by perfume alone, so they use advertising to make people feel good when they buy and use them.

Some brands depend on their owned media for success. Clothes retailer Zara invests in premium storefronts in prime locations to showcase its products, and Krispy Kreme lets its well-placed, eye-catching cabinets and tempting donuts do all the talking.

If a brand is appealing, highly differentiated from its competition and delivers a satisfying user experience, it may be able to grow thanks to earned media alone. Brands as diverse as Rolls-Royce and Costco rely on word of mouth to attract customers rather than investing in paid media. If earned media alone cannot stimulate a trial fast enough, sampling can be highly effective.

The media priority matrix helps determine the best type of media to use based on the brand's user experience and the level of risk associated with the purchase.

MEDIA PRIORITY MATRIX

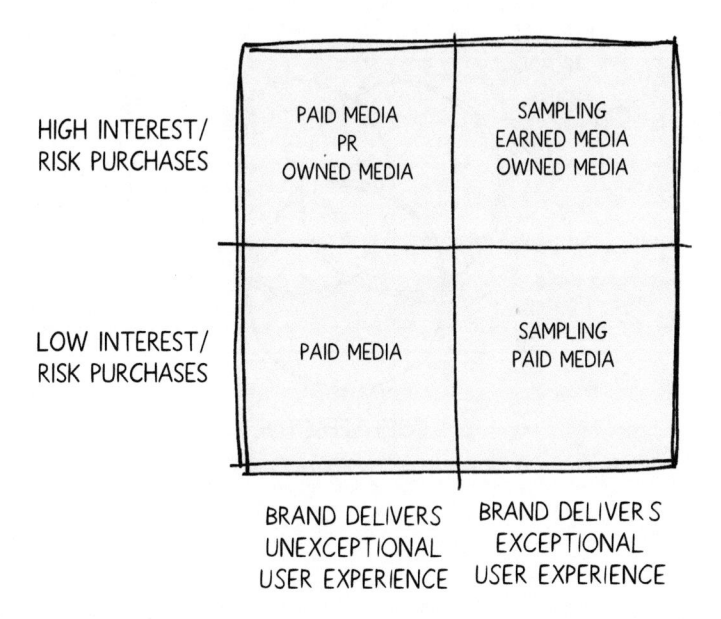

	BRAND DELIVERS UNEXCEPTIONAL USER EXPERIENCE	BRAND DELIVERS EXCEPTIONAL USER EXPERIENCE
HIGH INTEREST/ RISK PURCHASES	PAID MEDIA PR OWNED MEDIA	SAMPLING EARNED MEDIA OWNED MEDIA
LOW INTEREST/ RISK PURCHASES	PAID MEDIA	SAMPLING PAID MEDIA

The higher the risk, the more reassurance customers need, so PR or earned media may be needed as well as paid media. Brands with an exceptional user experience should exploit this by investing heavily in sampling and making sure praise for the brand is communicated as widely as possible.

When it comes to choosing specific media channels, brands can use three criteria: right for the brand, fits the creative idea and cost effective.

IDENTIFYING SPECIFIC MEDIA CHANNELS TO USE

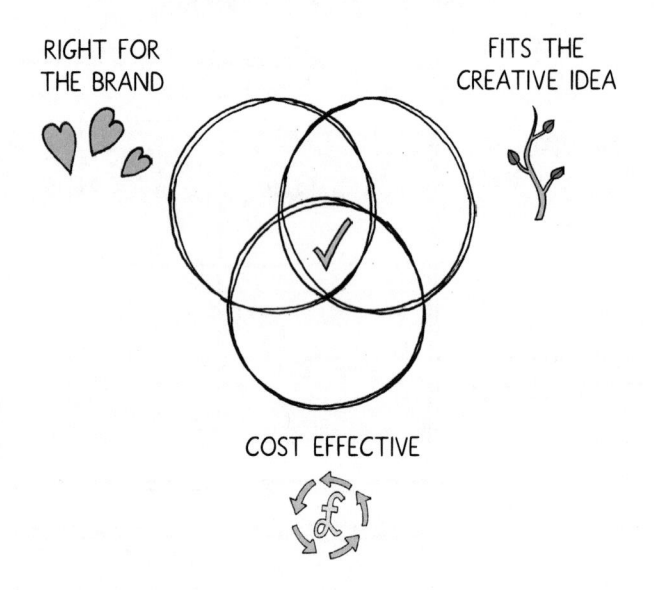

RIGHT FOR THE BRAND

FITS THE CREATIVE IDEA

COST EFFECTIVE

RIGHT FOR THE BRAND
The media should always reflect the brand's positioning. Red Bull's sponsorship of Formula 1 Racing, extreme sports events and challenge-themed PR activities, for example, all reinforce its identity as an exhilarating brand.

FITS THE CREATIVE IDEA
If a creative idea is already in place, some channels might be better suited to bringing it to life than others. An example of this is Bic placing a giant razor at the end of a mowed strip of grass beside a Japanese freeway as part of a campaign publicizing the brand's close shave.

COST EFFECTIVE
Media investment should only be considered if the profit (not revenue) from extra sales generated will exceed the total cost, including the time and money spent coming up with good ideas, producing content and achieving exposures.

CHANNEL COST VS PROFIT

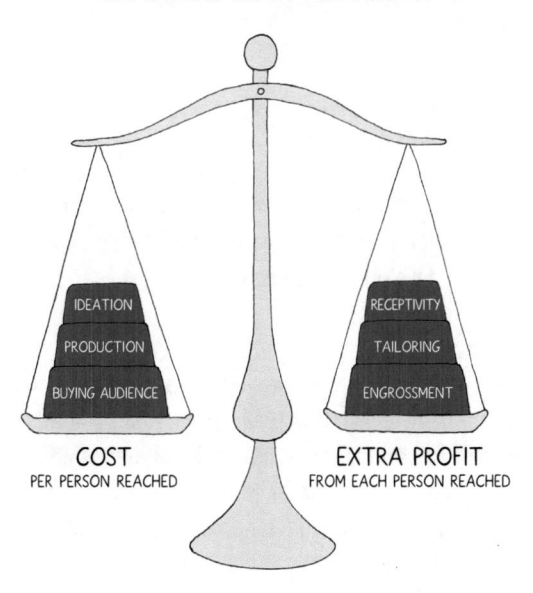

COST
PER PERSON REACHED
- IDEATION
- PRODUCTION
- BUYING AUDIENCE

EXTRA PROFIT
FROM EACH PERSON REACHED
- RECEPTIVITY
- TAILORING
- ENGROSSMENT

Calculating the extra profit can prove complicated but even rough estimations can prevent marketers from embarking on projects that could never pay back. Analytics can be applied to indicate the range of possible sales and profit gains for channels used previously or for which benchmark data is available. Often, however, marketers must use their judgment to decide whether a medium is worth the money, based on three factors: receptivity, tailoring and engrossment.

RECEPTIVITY

Communications are more effective if people are in the right frame of mind for the brand's message to resonate with them when they encounter it. A low-alcohol beer, for example, might need to advertise on subway escalators to catch commuters as they travel home, looking forward to relaxing in the evening but aware of their early start the next day.

TAILORING

Most digital media allow different content to be served to different consumer segments, defined in increasingly nuanced ways. This can greatly enhance the impact of the communications if enough is known about each segment, they vary significantly, and there is time and money to develop tailored content.

ENGROSSMENT

Some forms of media are inherently more engrossing than others, and this is largely reflected in their prices. A small roadside poster has a limited opportunity to captivate its audience compared to a two-minute cinema ad. However, the degree to which a brand capitalizes on a channel's potential for engagement depends heavily on the creativity of its content.

5.4 CHANNEL ROLES AND CONNECTIONS

When choosing media, it can be helpful to consider the two complementary roles they can play. Media can create interest and credibility for a brand by building mental associations that last for years – a concept called brand development. These make people more predisposed to the brand but may not be enough to deliver sales on their own. People are bombarded with so much marketing that it is often necessary to remind consumers of the brand close to the purchase decision and bring its associations to the fore so they can work their magic – i.e., activation. This is why an effective combination of long-term brand development media and short-term activation media is widely used. In other words, brand-building media put the ball in the vicinity of the goal, and activation media put it in the back of the net.

BRAND DEVELOPMENT & ACTIVATION

ACTIVATION
e.g., posters near outlets, in-store activities, paid search

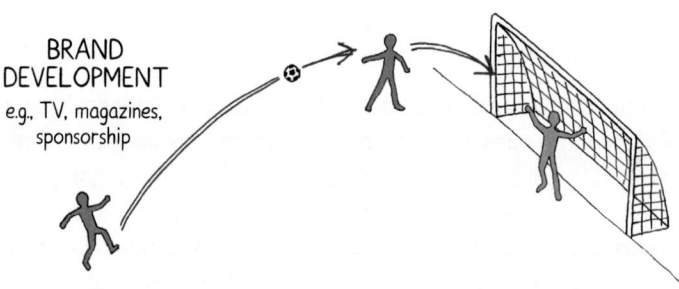

BRAND DEVELOPMENT
e.g., TV, magazines, sponsorship

Marketers should be clear about which communications channels they will use for brand development and which for activation. At the same time, they should specify how channels combine to influence purchase decisions.

CHANNEL CONNECTIONS ILLUSTRATION

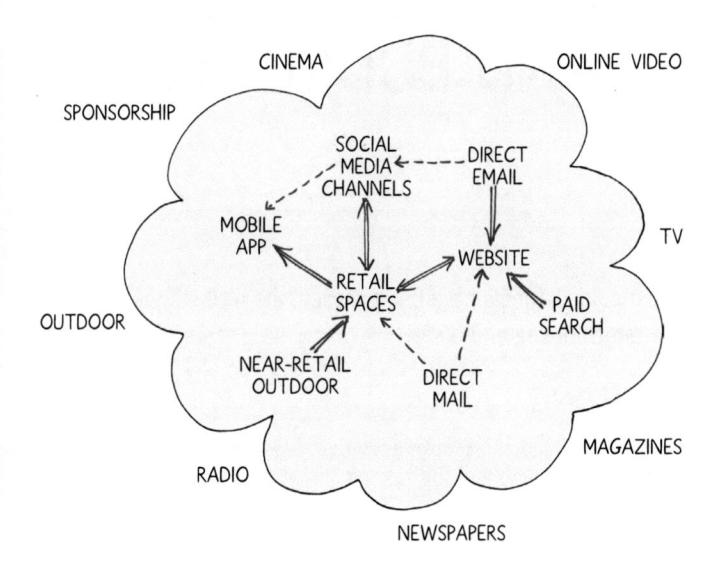

In this illustration, the outer brand development channels create a cloud of positive predisposition around the brand, making people more responsive to the inner activation channels. For example, TV creates interest in the brand, making people click on the ad that appears when they search for the category, and this takes them straight to the brand's website.

5.5 MEDIA PLANNING AND BUDGETING

Once media channels have been chosen, the next step is to determine target, timing and budget.

TARGETING
Depending on the budget available, communications should either be aimed at the whole of the brand's target or a subset known to be more receptive to the brand or the specific product currently in focus.

TIMING

MEDIA PLAN ILLUSTRATION

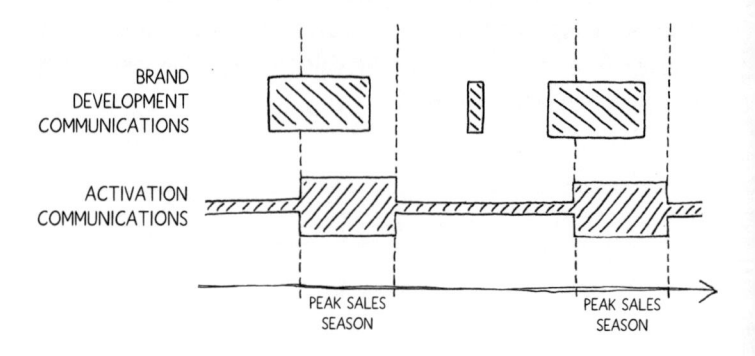

BRAND DEVELOPMENT COMMUNICATIONS	▨	▫	▨
ACTIVATION COMMUNICATIONS	▨		▨
	PEAK SALES SEASON		PEAK SALES SEASON

The diagram on the previous page highlights key principles of communications timing:

- Brand development is concentrated just before and during peak category sales periods (if there are any)
- Brands should avoid long spells (e.g., three months or more) without brand development because it takes more to re-establish memories if they have been allowed to fade for long
- Activation communications (e.g., paid search) should be continuous so that potential customers are reminded of the brand and its benefits just before they buy, whenever that may be
- Spending on activation communications is increased during peak periods, especially if there are sales promotions to publicize

If there isn't a reason for concentrating spending at certain times, such as sales seasonality or a product launch, media should be spread out over time to increase efficiency ('drip' rather than 'burst').

BURST VS DRIP

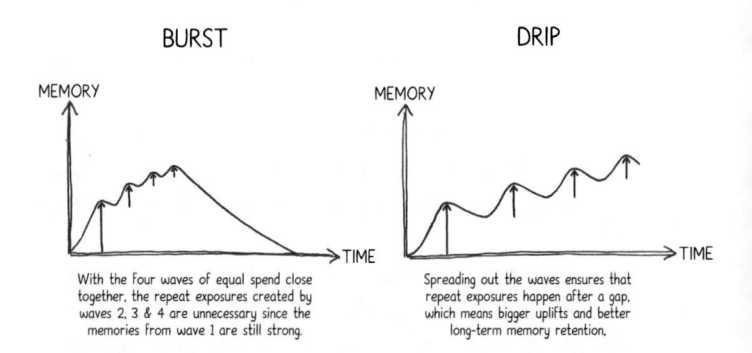

BURST

With the four waves of equal spend close together, the repeat exposures created by waves 2, 3 & 4 are unnecessary since the memories from wave 1 are still strong.

DRIP

Spreading out the waves ensures that repeat exposures happen after a gap, which means bigger uplifts and better long-term memory retention.

REACH VS FREQUENCY

The sales impact of one exposure compared to none is greater than the impact of ten versus nine. This diminishing returns effect means that communications plans should prioritize reach over frequency. The effect is reduced with multiple executions within a channel and using multiple channels with non-overlapping audiences is a good way to reach more people and keep frequencies down. The golden rule is to avoid people being exposed to the same content many times within a short time frame (e.g., 10 to 15 times in a week) especially if the content relies on a 'punchline' or is slightly irritating to start with.

ALLOCATING SPENDING TO CHANNELS

Priority should be given to channels believed to meet the communications objectives at the lowest cost. However, because of diminishing returns, the spending on any channel should be kept below the level at which it stops being a good investment.

DIMINISHING RETURNS FROM MEDIA SPEND

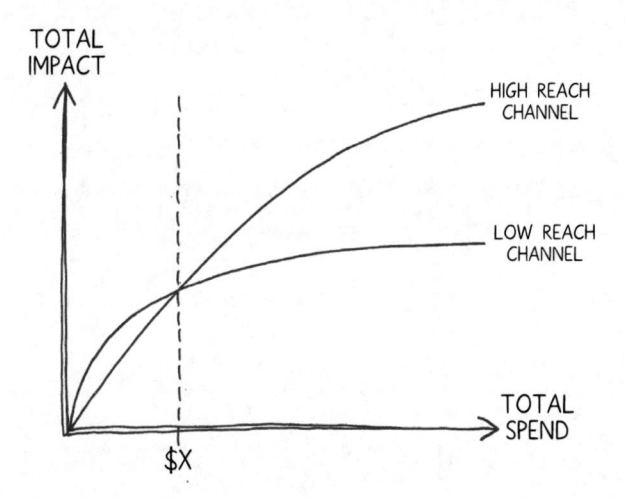

In the typical scenario illustrated here, a brand should use the low reach channel if the budget is less than $X and the high reach channel if the spend is more than $X. The most efficient option, however, is a mix of the two channels, especially if their audiences do not overlap much.

PART **SIX**

COMMUNICATIONS CONTENT

WHAT PEOPLE REMEMBER

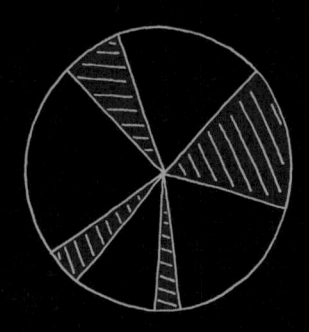

CREATIVE CONTENT

6.1 GENERATING A COMMUNICATIONS IDEA

A communications idea is a theme that runs through all of a brand's communications and helps the brand develop a clear, coherent set of brand associations. The Snickers brand, for example, used the idea of showing people acting like divas when they're hungry, then returning to normal once they've eaten a Snickers bar. The insight behind this was that people's temperament often changes temporarily when their blood sugar levels are low. The 'diva' idea was one way of using this insight in order to reinforce the purpose of the brand – to fill people up when they're hungry – and was used as the basis for multiple executions across multiple channels for many years. Great communications ideas like this resonate with the target audience and highlight the brand's purpose.

GENERATING GREAT COMMUNICATION IDEAS

CONSUMERS' CONCERNS

The audience's needs and desires, related to the category and beyond

EUREKA!

BRAND PURPOSE

What the brand stands for – how it seeks to enhance people's lives

A workshop involving the brand team and, if possible, external creative experts is ideal for coming up with strong communications ideas. Attendees should aim to develop a strong sympathetic understanding of the target audience before or at the start of the workshop. Most useful for this would be information and insights about how, when and why target consumers use the category and about their lifestyles, attitudes and priorities more generally. The goal of the workshop is to develop ideas that relate to a consumer concern and allow the brand to play a 'hero' role.

Once a winning idea has been identified, the next step is to brief a creative team to come up with executions for whichever media are being used. Agencies may have a preferred way to be briefed but, as a guide, the brief should include the following, as outlined in the following illustration.

BRIEFING CREATIVES

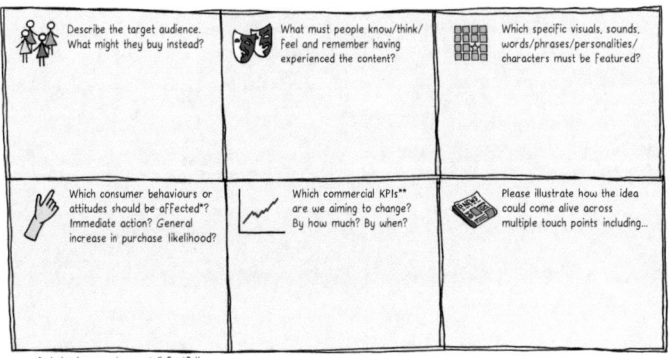

Describe the target audience. What might they buy instead?	What must people know/think/feel and remember having experienced the content?	Which specific visuals, sounds, words/phrases/personalities/characters must be featured?
Which consumer behaviours or attitudes should be affected*? Immediate action? General increase in purchase likelihood?	Which commercial KPIs** are we aiming to change? By how much? By when?	Please illustrate how the idea could come alive across multiple touch points including...

* behaviours such as retail footfall, applications, number of test drives, website visits, and attitudinal metrics such as brand salience/awareness, or consideration.

**e.g. increases in sales/subscriptions, market share or profit.

To help fire the imagination of the creative team, it helps if the brief itself is creative. It's important to convey what the target audience is really like and to specify any distinctive brand assets that must be featured in the executions. Assets could be visuals, sounds, words, phrases, personalities or characters – anything designed to help the brand be remembered and differentiated from competitors. It's also helpful at the briefing stage to ask for examples of how the idea could be used across multiple channels to make sure it has the flexibility the brand needs.

6.2 ASSESSING CREATIVE IDEAS

The following framework is helpful when assessing the potential of creative ideas.

IDEAS THAT LEAD TO GREAT COMMUNICATIONS

- RESONATE EMOTIONALLY
- A ROLE FOR THE BRAND
- RELEVANT ASSOCIATIONS
- DISTINCTIVE ASSETS
- GENERATE DISCUSSION
- INSPIRE CREATIVTY
- EASILY ADAPTED

RESONATE EMOTIONALLY
Striking a chord with the audience is paramount. People understand and identify with the best ideas effortlessly. Creating an emotional connection means people will remember the communications and see the brand in a positive light.

A ROLE FOR THE BRAND
Some communications ideas fail because people find them hard to connect with the brand. The brand should be so central to the idea that when people describe the idea, they naturally refer to the brand. The brand purpose, if there is one, usually provides the connection between the brand and the idea.

RELEVANT ASSOCIATIONS
The idea should evoke the kind of associations desired for the brand. For example, advertising for Snuggle fabric softener for many years featured an animated teddy bear who loved cosying up to fresh laundry and this connected the brand to the concepts of softness and family loving care.

DISTINCTIVE ASSETS
A distinctive asset is anything associated with the brand in people's minds and not associated with other brands. These could be visuals, sounds, words, phrases, personalities or characters. The Nike 'swoosh' and 'Just Do It' slogan are two examples. Once established, featuring distinctive assets in communications will help bring the brand to mind when the communications are experienced. This helps the formation of new associations or the reinforcement of existing ones.

GENERATE DISCUSSION
The impact of a campaign can be greatly magnified if it is socially relevant. The #likeagirl campaign by sanitary products brand Always encouraged people to reflect on how using the phrase derogatively could damage girls' self-confidence. The campaign generated lots of media attention, became a hot topic on social media (177,000 tweets featuring the hashtag in three months) and had a phenomenal impact on sales.

INSPIRE CREATIVITY
A sure sign that an idea has potential is if the team can easily find lots of ways of bringing the idea to life across different channels. Some the most effective campaigns have even inspired brand fans to create their own iterations or parodies. Coca-Cola's 'Share a Coke' campaign prompted the sharing of hundreds of thousands of pictures showing Coke bottles spelling out witty phrases – and even one or two marriage proposals.

EASILY ADAPTED
Communications ideas should be universal enough to work across different media and cultures. If an idea is so rigid and specific that it only works in one channel, it probably isn't a big enough idea to be compelling for the audience.

6.3 ASSESSING PIECES OF CONTENT

Weeding out content with little potential and investing only in the best saves money and ensures communications achieve greater impact. To do this, content should be assessed at every stage of the development process, ideally guided by market research and based on the criteria below.

ASSESSING COMMUNICATIONS CONTENT

WHAT TO LOOK FOR

COMMAND ATTENTION
Does it draw attention?
Does it quickly create interest or emotion?

FORGE BRAND ASSOCIATIONS
What will people actually remember?
Will the brand be part of this?
Will the desired associations be made?

INFLUENCE DECISIONS
Do people feel it's relevant to them?
Do they find it credible?
Does it make the brand appealing?

ENHANCE USER SATISFACTION
Does it evoke the benefits of using the brand?
Does it make the brand's offer seem unique?

People don't have the mental capacity to take in everything going on around them, so they are wired to ignore most of it and only attend to anything out of the ordinary, in case it represents a danger or new opportunity. This means that content needs to stand out from the environment and be distinctive in order to grab attention. It then needs to quickly connect with the audience intellectually or emotionally in order to hold attention. Ways of doing this include posing a question or featuring attractive people, adorable animals, captivating imagery or stirring music.

Once attention has been gained, people retain whatever they find most engaging and forget the rest. It's not uncommon for less than half of an audiovisual ad to be recalled minutes after being seen, and when it comes to feelings, people tend to only remember the strongest emotion they felt and the emotion they were left with at the end.

SELECTIVE ATTENTION

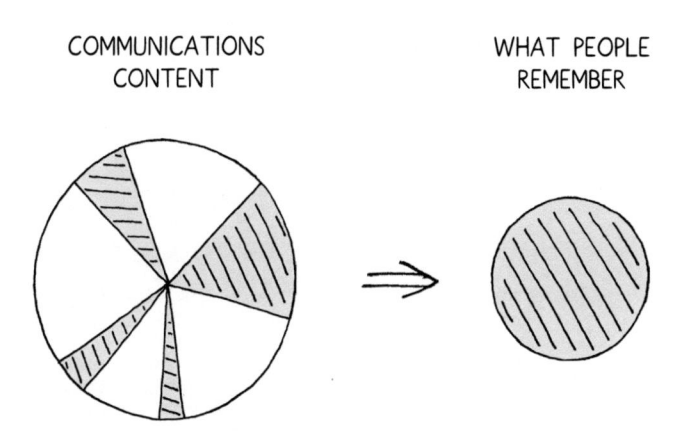

COMMUNICATIONS CONTENT

WHAT PEOPLE REMEMBER

Market research can help predict what will be remembered in the long run. For content to be effective, whatever is retained needs to conjure the desired associations and be connected to the brand.

If the strategy is sound, the content should feel relevant to the audience, credible for the brand and create positive feelings toward the brand. Brand appeal or consideration are appropriate measures, but purchase intent is not because purchase decisions depend on other factors, such as trying out the product and how it is priced compared to alternatives.

Communications have an even greater impact if they make people appreciate the brand more when they use it, so the best content brings the user experience alive in a memorable way and makes it seem unique.

A good way to predict if content is likely to stay in people's memory is to consider the ways it could trigger psychological processes in the brain. There are three types of long-term memory (episodic, semantic and procedural), and content ideally goes into two or even all three.

TYPES OF LONG-TERM MEMORY

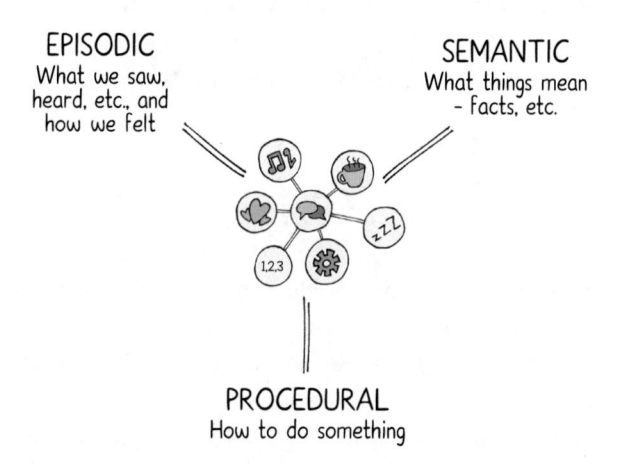

EPISODIC
What we saw, heard, etc., and how we felt

SEMANTIC
What things mean – facts, etc.

PROCEDURAL
How to do something

EPISODIC
These are images, sounds and feelings remembered from the content. Communications that tell stories are good at creating episodic memories because people find stories easy to understand and remember while also engaging with them emotionally.

SEMANTIC
Semantic memories are concerned with meaning. These include what a product does, its features and benefits.

PROCEDURAL
Procedural memories relate to how actions are performed. Showing ways of using a product ensures procedural memories are created. Oreo biscuits feature the 'Twist, Lick, Dunk' ritual in their communications and have used it to launch the brand all over the world.

6.4 THE IMPORTANCE OF BRANDING

A common failing of communications content is people being unable to remember the brand or, worse still, attributing it to a competitor. Careful thought should be given to making it easy for people to register the brand. Not every detail will be remembered from an ad, but the brand should never be left on the mental cutting-room floor.

Here are some ways to ensure a clear role for the brand.

ENSURING A CLEAR ROLE FOR THE BRAND

STARRING ROLE

AGENT OF CHANGE

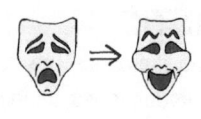

BENEFACTOR

UNIQUE DESIGN OWNER

STARRING ROLE
The brand is sure to be remembered if the product itself is distinctive and it takes a leading role in the communications (e.g., Dyson), or a character who personifies the brand (e.g., Cillit Bang's Barry Scott) is the star.

AGENT OF CHANGE
If the brand plays a pivotal role in transforming a situation from bad to good (e.g., Snickers), it is likely to be remembered. This 'problem-solution' advertising format is long established and still works well if it is executed in an original way.

BENEFACTOR
Another way for a brand to be recognized is as the benefactor or sponsor for content the target audience loves. This works if the brand is routinely mentioned in connection with the content. For example, from 1996 to 2017, Virgin brought music and comedy to audiences in the UK via the 'V Festival' each summer, which reinforced the brand's adventurous, passionate and creative personality.

UNIQUE DESIGN OWNER
Owning a distinctive design style is a huge benefit for a brand. It means that content using the style will be immediately recognized and connected with the brand (e.g., Red Bull 'Gives You Wings'). This is why some brands identify a set of distinctive assets that will be featured in all the brand's advertising. By using the same assets time and again, they become strongly associated with the brand. When featured in communications, these assets immediately bring the brand to mind, making it easy for new associations to be created. Establishing the associations is the same as how

Pavlov's dogs learned to connect the sound of a bell with feeding time. It just requires them to coincide multiple times.

Distinctive brand assets are especially valuable because they can also be used to trigger brand memories and influence decisions near to the purchase moment, e.g., by featuring them on the pack itself or in point-of-sale activity. The distinctive purple colour of a Cadbury bar triggers Cadbury associations as soon as people see it.

6.5 OPTIMIZING CONTENT

It's always worth optimizing content based on consumer feedback, especially if the media budget is high.

CONTENT IMPROVEMENT FLOW DIAGRAM

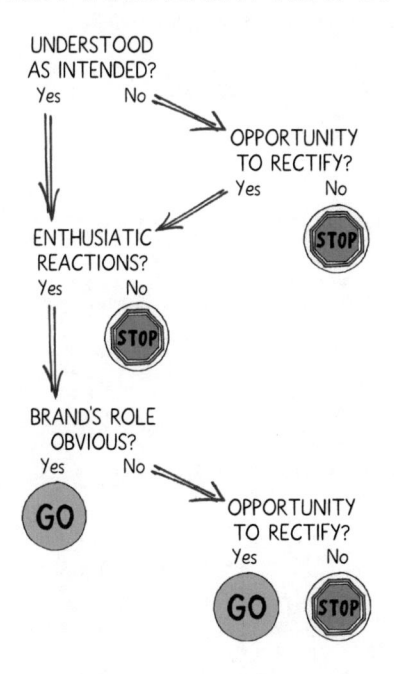

- UNDERSTOOD AS INTENDED?
  - Yes → ENTHUSIATIC REACTIONS?
  - No → OPPORTUNITY TO RECTIFY?
    - Yes → ENTHUSIATIC REACTIONS?
    - No → STOP
- ENTHUSIATIC REACTIONS?
  - Yes → BRAND'S ROLE OBVIOUS?
  - No → STOP
- BRAND'S ROLE OBVIOUS?
  - Yes → GO
  - No → OPPORTUNITY TO RECTIFY?
    - Yes → GO
    - No → STOP

The first thing to check is whether people understand the content as intended. It's easy for the development team to be so close to the project that they assume too much knowledge on the part of the audience. Small changes can often solve comprehension problems and unleash the power of the idea.

If the idea is understood but people's reactions are underwhelming, the content most likely lacks potential and the focus should be shifted to alternatives.

If reactions are positive, the final check is to ensure that the brand's role is clear. If it isn't, might be possible to strengthen the brand connection by making it more explicit or increasing the brand's prominence within the memorable elements.

There are several ways content could be improved, provided the underlying idea is good.

IMPROVING COMMUNICATIONS CONTENT

SHOWCASE THE 'HOOK'

REDUCE THE CLUTTER

DIRECT PEOPLE'S ATTENTION

FOCUS ON ONE MESSAGE

SHOWCASE THE HOOK
Grabbing attention is vital, so whichever element is most engaging – the 'hook' – should be given centre stage. This could be a strikingly designed product, an intriguing visual, a surprising headline or some stirring music.

REDUCE THE CLUTTER
Content can often be improved by making it simpler and removing the clutter. Visual ads that look crowded tend to be passed by. Likewise, people switch off if they're watching video content that's hard to follow or overloaded with information. Ads with a continuous voiceover, for example, quickly lose people's attention. Providing downtime within an ad allows ideas and messages to sink in properly, avoiding what's known as 'memory displacement.'

DIRECT PEOPLE'S ATTENTION
People instinctively focus on certain salient elements: human faces, where those faces are looking, strong contrasting colours and movement. This knowledge can be used to direct attention to the brand or other vital elements of the content. It can also be used to remove distractions that are diverting attention from something important.

FOCUS ON ONE MESSAGE
In terms of messaging, best practice is to focus on just one or two explicit messages within a single piece of content. Additional messages are unlikely to be recalled and may leave audiences confused and disinterested. The most effective content keeps explicit messaging to a minimum and provides breathing space for powerful implicit communications via imagery, music, characters and storyline.

PART **SEVEN**

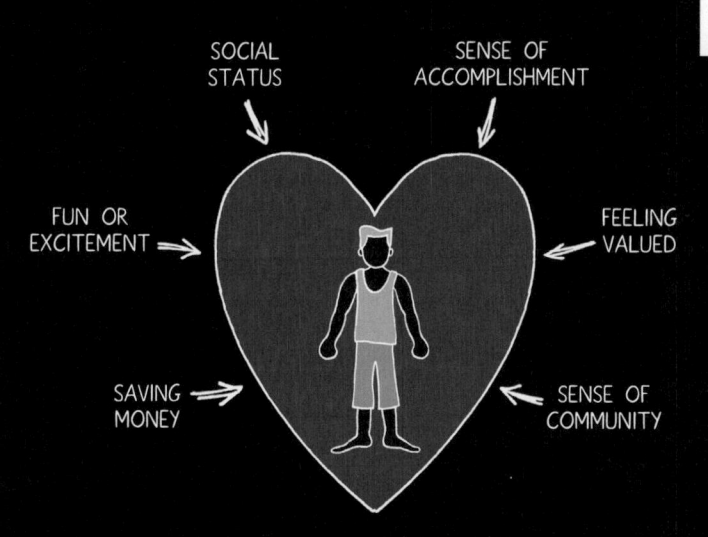

SOCIAL STATUS

SENSE OF ACCOMPLISHMENT

FUN OR EXCITEMENT

FEELING VALUED

SAVING MONEY

SENSE OF COMMUNITY

SALES PROMOTION

7.1 WHEN TO ADJUST PRICING

Managing price is a crucial element of the marketing mix because it can have a profound impact on both short- and long-term profit.

According to the *Harvard Business Review* (1992), a company typically experiences an 11% drop in operating profits from a price reduction of just 1%; McKinsey & Co (2003) quoted a similar figure of 8%. It is clear that maintaining a brand's price is critical to long-term profitability.

However, price adjustments can help a company to manage its cash flow by boosting sales during quieter periods or optimizing profits when supply is limited. In most markets, low-priced brands sell at higher volumes than high-priced brands, and a brand will sell more if it drops its price and sell less if it raises it. The brand's price relative to its most direct competitors is usually the most important consideration, so marketers should keep a close eye on pricing and make adjustments to keep the difference within an acceptable range. The range itself depends on the appeal of the brand compared to its close competitors.

APPEAL VERSUS PRICE TRADE-OFF

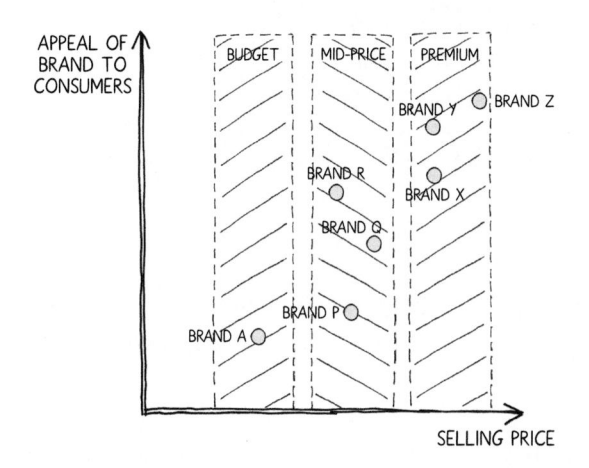

In the illustration, Brand A is the only budget brand, so is likely to be chosen by anyone looking for the lowest-priced option. Brand P is in a bad position because its price is similar to Brands Q and R, but it is much less appealing. Brand R has a clear advantage over Brand Q because it is more appealing to consumers but priced slightly lower. In the premium sector, Brand Y beats Brand X because it holds greater appeal for the same price, while Brand Z is likely to appeal to anyone who wants the very best the category has to offer and is prepared to pay for it.

Given that consumers think in this way, the optimum price of a brand depends on the prices of its closest competitors. As a consequence of this, companies tend to follow each other's pricing, which can lead to 'price wars' in which value is driven out of the category until most companies struggle to make a profit. The survivors are brands with high differentiation and appeal because these are under less pressure to drop their prices.

7.2 WHEN TO USE PRICE PROMOTIONS

Price promotions involve reducing the selling price for a limited period or removing other fees the customer normally pays, such as shipping.

While potentially relevant to low- and mid-priced brands, there is clear evidence that premium brands should avoid discounting in this way. Higher price signals higher quality to the consumer, an effect explained by expectancy theory, so price reductions undermine perceptions of quality and exclusivity. This explains why luxury brand Louis Vuitton rewards its employees with unsold stock each season, rather than damage its image by selling it off at a discount.

Retailers sometimes ask that brands offer price promotions as a condition for stocking them. The brand owner can accept this as a cost of doing business but if the brand is highly differentiated and popular with consumers, it is in a much stronger position to negotiate. If price promotions are necessary, marketers need to know how to deploy them in the best way possible.

PRICE PROMOTION GOLDEN RULES

DON'T GIVE IT AWAY

DO THE SUMS

FIND AN EXCUSE

KEEP IT SHORT

MAKE IT A RARITY

DON'T GIVE IT AWAY
The appropriate level of discount depends on the norms and economics of the category, but the aim is to identify the sweet spot: enough of a reduction to attract consumers' attention but not so much as to damage the brand's reputation.

DO THE SUMS
The main cost of running a price promotion is the reduction in profit from purchases that would have happened at full price without the promotion, but there will also be costs from organizing and publicizing the promotion. The net impact of the promotion on profit can easily be negative.

FIND AN EXCUSE
If a special reason can be found for offering a reduced price, such as celebrating the brand's birthday, this helps reinforce its rarity and help avoid diminishing the brand's quality credentials.

KEEP IT SHORT
People generally value things more if they are in short supply due to what's known as the scarcity heuristic and the fear of missing out (FOMO), which is why they're more likely to act on a promotion if it won't be available for long. This is why 'countdown' sales are so effective.

MAKE IT A RARITY
If price promotions occur frequently, customers learn to expect them. This devalues the brand and trains customers to only consider buying it when it's on offer. Price promotions should therefore be used sparingly.

If a business is struggling to keep the books balanced, promotions might offer a temporary solution. Slashing prices or offering generous volume discounts can help by boosting cash flow or by reducing the cost to the business of holding on to excess inventory. These kinds of promotion may be necessary to support a business's finances at key moments but should only be considered as a last resort.

7.3 PROMOTIONS TO BUILD THE CUSTOMER BASE

Sales promotions can play a vital role in helping build a brand's customer base, even if they cost more than the immediate return from the new sales generated. They can pay back many times over in the long run if the new customers buy the brand on future occasions at full price or buy other products from the brand. Brands with a great user experience stand to benefit the most because repeat purchase is likely. Brands like this should invest in sales promotions during their launch phase to kick-start their user base. Brands with a weak user experience achieve little from sales promotions apart from a short-lived spike in sales.

LIFETIME VALUE OF A HAPPY LOYAL CUSTOMER

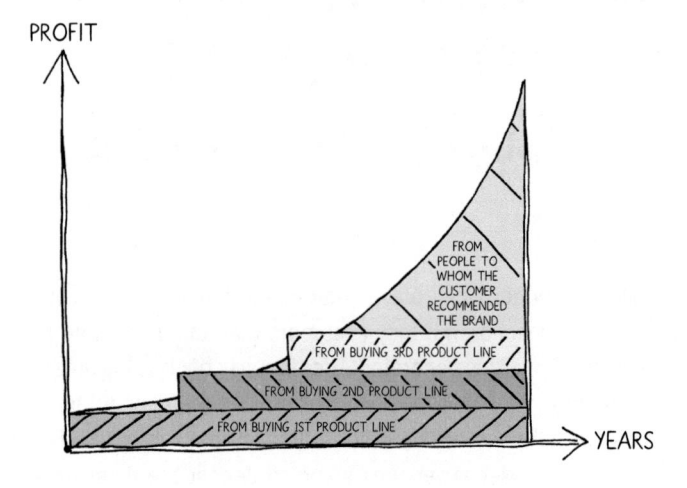

PROFIT

FROM PEOPLE TO WHOM THE CUSTOMER RECOMMENDED THE BRAND

FROM BUYING 3RD PRODUCT LINE

FROM BUYING 2ND PRODUCT LINE

FROM BUYING 1ST PRODUCT LINE

YEARS

Promotions and incentives are especially valuable for influencing people who are actively considering the brand. A small incentive can often be enough to precipitate their decision and sway it in the brand's favour. Giving away something for free works well, especially if potential customers value it more than it costs the business to provide. The freebie could be a small gift, the delivery charge or a warranty that normally costs extra. Offering money off the customer's next purchase is a good strategy because it encourages customers to buy the brand a second time, giving the product another chance to impress. The same thinking applies to subscription-based brands. Reducing or removing the fee for new subscribers during an introductory period gives the brand a chance to prove its value. Also, once consumers are using the brand, they will value it more due to a bias known as the endowment effect. They will also be reluctant to let the brand go due to loss aversion.

Companies that own multiple products or brands have cross-promotion opportunities. The sales promotion for one product can be used to generate interest in another. For example, the incentive could be a free trial or discount voucher for another product.

In categories where making a purchase is a big decision due to the high cost or the risk of making a bad choice (e.g., switching current accounts), sales promotions can be used to make the decision less daunting.

MAKING DIFFICULT PURCHASES EASIER

EXTENDED WARRANTIES

TRY BEFORE YOU BUY

FEE-FREE SWITCHING

7.4 PROMOTIONS TO ATTRACT LAPSED BUYERS

In competitive, fast-moving categories where consumers have lots of almost equally attractive choices, even good brands can find it hard to hold on to regular customers and be noticed among the clutter. In these categories, brands need to exploit every opportunity to grab consumers' attention and remind consumers what they're missing. Success depends on continually attracting new customers and triggering lapsed and occasional buyers to buy again to compensate for the ongoing defection of buyers to competitors.

CONTINUALLY FILLING THE LEAKY BUCKET

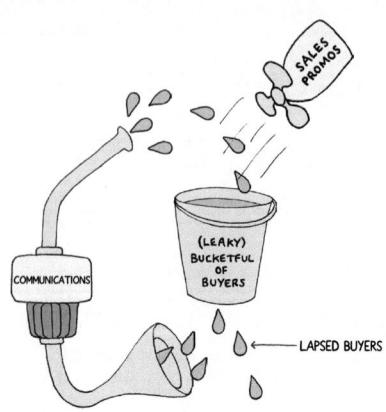

Sales promotions can be an effective way to achieve sales from people who would otherwise have overlooked the brand, especially when used in conjunction with brand-building communications. The communications make people receptive to the brand, so sales promotions just need to close the deal.

Best practices for sales promotions aimed at lapsed buyers are described below.

USE MODEST INCENTIVES

Since the objective is to remind people about a brand they already like, a small incentive should be sufficient. Options include a modest price discount, a free taster of another product or a reward that all buyers of the product are currently receiving, such as a free prize draw. Deep discounts should be avoided.

AVOID JUST REACHING HEAVY BUYERS

Sales promotions designed for lapsed buyers can easily backfire if regular buyers are the ones who end up taking advantage of them. The promotion needs to be open to everyone but will be more cost-effective if the publicity can be targeted at people who haven't bought the brand for a while and have been buying competitor brands instead. Promotions that only regular buyers are likely to see, such as discounts advertised on the shelf, should be avoided.

REFLECT THE BRAND'S POSITIONING
Using a theme that's in keeping with the brand image reminds people what's good about the brand, which encourages them to buy. It also helps to strengthen brand associations among everyone who sees the promotion, not just those taking advantage of it. To maximize effectiveness, the theme, style and messaging should be aligned with any other communications being used by the brand.

GET PEOPLE INVOLVED
Some of the most effective promotions ask people to do something in return for a reward, such as posting a selfie that reflects the theme of the promotion along with the appropriate hashtag. Participation like this makes the promotion more memorable and helps keep the brand at the top of the mind for longer.

COLLECT CONTACT INFORMATION AND PERMISSION
Sales promotions are a good way to build up a database of potential customers, which can be used for direct marketing campaigns. To make this possible, participants should be asked to follow the brand on social media or provide contact information.

7.5 SCHEMES TO ENHANCE RETENTION

Brands grow if they gain more customers over time than they lose, so it makes good business sense to find cost-effective ways of enhancing customer retention.

Loyalty schemes encourage customers to stick with the brand and make the prospect of switching allegiances unattractive. The most effective schemes come from knowing what target customers like and expect from the brand and the kinds of practical or emotional reward they'd appreciate in return for their loyalty.

REWARDING LOYAL CUSTOMERS

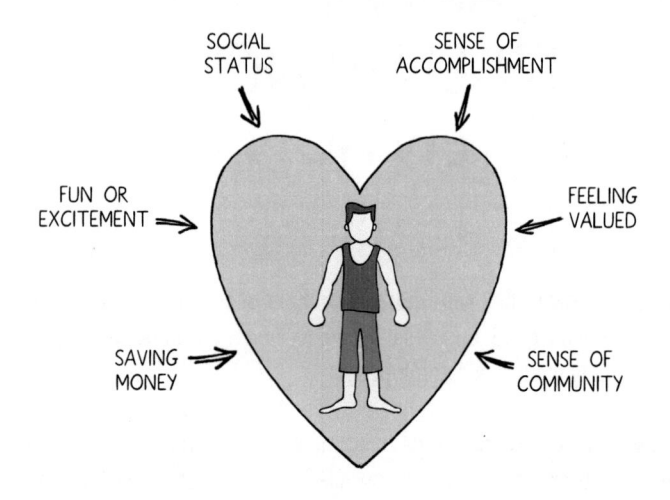

- SOCIAL STATUS
- SENSE OF ACCOMPLISHMENT
- FUN OR EXCITEMENT
- FEELING VALUED
- SAVING MONEY
- SENSE OF COMMUNITY

SAVING MONEY

This is particularly relevant if the brand's appeal comes from providing value for money. Many retailers' loyalty programmes provide discounts in return for points accumulated as customers spend more. Coffee shops encourage customers to choose them by routinely offering a free drink after a certain number of visits.

FUN OR EXCITEMENT

If appropriate for the brand's positioning, fun activities such as competitions or events are ideal rewards. In its early days, smoothie producer Innocent invited its fans to a free festival each summer called 'Fruitstock.' Even small elements of fun incorporated into a promotion can work well, such as spinning a virtual wheel for a bonus discount or free prize.

SOCIAL STATUS
US beauty brand Sephora helps customers build their social status through its loyalty programme. When members reach certain spend thresholds each calendar year, they progress to higher tiers granting increasingly prestigious perks. 'VIB Rouge' status gains access to a private beauty advisor hotline, free express shipping and invitations to exclusive events that lend themselves to enviable social media updates.

SENSE OF ACCOMPLISHMENT
If people have to accrue their privileges through multiple purchases or longevity as a customer, they tend to be reluctant to let them go due to a psychological effect called loss aversion. With the Sky VIP programme, it takes 15 years to reach the 'Diamond' level, which provides queue-free access to customer support on top of all the other perks accumulated as a member of lower tiers.

FEELING VALUED
Providing complementary services is a good way to make loyal customers feel valued. Upmarket UK supermarket chain Waitrose gives its regular customers a copy of their lifestyle magazine and a coffee whenever they shop, while airlines typically reward their most frequent flyers with free upgrades.

SENSE OF COMMUNITY
Purpose-driven brands are well placed to build a community that customers value and enjoy being a part of. For example, Pampers uses its websites and social media accounts to connect with parents around baby-related topics and provide expert advice and practical support.

PART **EIGHT**

SIMILAR USES/NEEDS   SIMILAR OR BETTER PRICE

MAJOR THREAT

INNOVATIVE MARKETING APPROACH

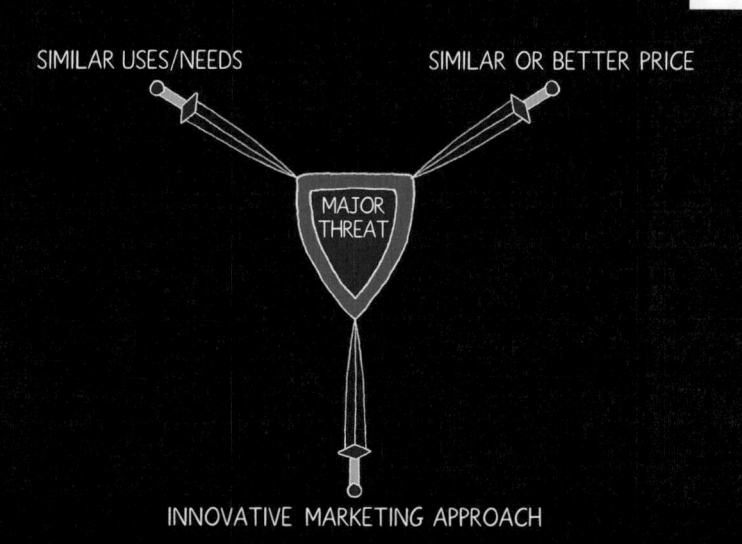

MEASUREMENT

8.1 USING DATA TO DRIVE MARKETING DECISIONS

Consumer understanding has always been a valuable input to business decision-making, but since the advent of digital technology, it has become vital. Digitization has opened up new ways to reach, make transactions with and distribute to consumers, and this has led to greater competition and consumer buying power. Meanwhile, social media has allowed people to share opinions about products and services, making word of mouth increasingly influential. With consumers having so much power, organizations need to exploit consumer data to deliver more relevant messages to different audiences and provide better experiences to their customers in order to remain competitive.

USING DATA & INSIGHTS TO INCREASE SALES & REDUCE COSTS

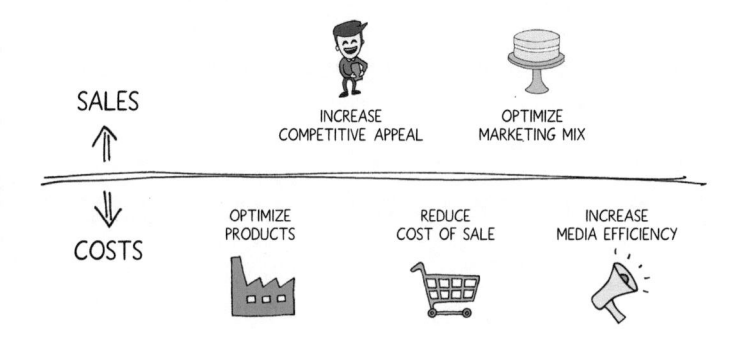

SALES ⇑

INCREASE COMPETITIVE APPEAL

OPTIMIZE MARKETING MIX

COSTS ⇓

OPTIMIZE PRODUCTS

REDUCE COST OF SALE

INCREASE MEDIA EFFICIENCY

INCREASE COMPETITIVE APPEAL
Research ensures that products and their communications reflect what customers find most appealing and are happy to pay for.

OPTIMIZE MARKETING MIX
Use consumer data to identify which elements of the marketing mix should be prioritized to help unlock sales.

OPTIMIZE PRODUCTS
Gaining an understanding of what consumers do and don't value helps during the development of new products and services. For example, features that have been identified as having little value to consumers can be ditched early in the process to save costs.

REDUCE COST OF SALE
Identifying the sales channels and activities with greatest impact at the lowest cost saves money.

INCREASE MEDIA EFFICIENCY
Revealing communications channels that improve sales at the lowest cost ensures optimum use of the media budget.

The contribution market research can make varies by where on the planning cycle the organization is currently.

M.R.'S ROLE THROUGH THE PLANNING CYCLE

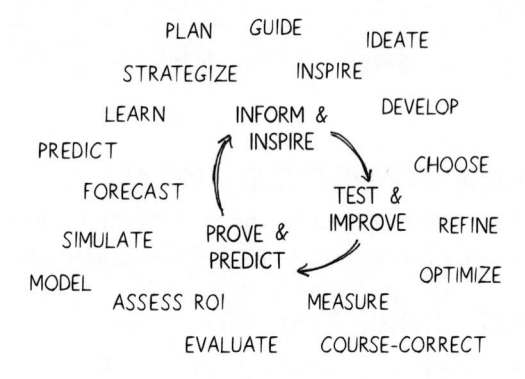

```
           PLAN    GUIDE       IDEATE
        STRATEGIZE     INSPIRE
     LEARN      INFORM &    DEVELOP
   PREDICT      INSPIRE
     FORECAST              CHOOSE
                    TEST &
     SIMULATE    PROVE &  IMPROVE   REFINE
                 PREDICT
     MODEL                        OPTIMIZE
          ASSESS ROI     MEASURE
           EVALUATE    COURSE-CORRECT
```

At the planning stage, market research provides insights into consumers' lives that guide and inspire the strategy. When ideas have been created, consumer feedback informs product development and helps identify promising ideas and how they could be improved. The best ideas can then be tested and optimized before going live. Once live, the effectiveness of new products and communications can be measured, course corrections made, and their overall return on investment evaluated. The data gathered can be used to predict whether future investment is worth the money and to learn which strategies are more effective and worth repeating.

8.2 MEASURING BRAND PROGRESS

Measuring brand progress allows a marketer to gauge how well the brand strategy is working, the impact marketing activity is having and to keep an eye on the competition. The four measures below are among the most important for gauging brand success.

MEASURING BRAND PROGRESS

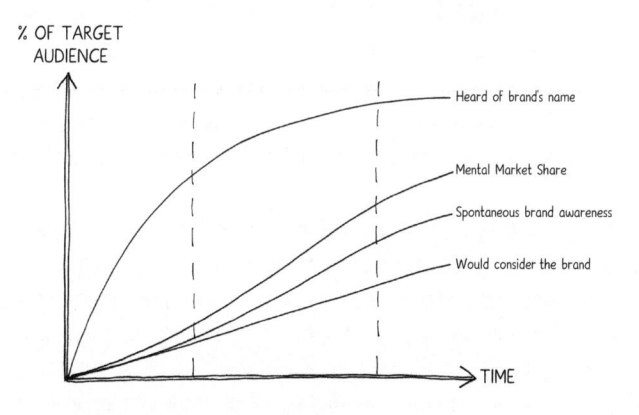

% OF TARGET AUDIENCE

- Heard of brand's name
- Mental Market Share
- Spontaneous brand awareness
- Would consider the brand

→ TIME

These dimensions tend to develop at different rates, which means that the most relevant measures of brand progress depend on the brand's life stage (see Section 5.2).

During the launch phase, awareness of the brand's name is a key metric. Familiarity with the brand name alone makes people more comfortable with the idea of buying it (due to the mere exposure effect).

During the expansion phase, the brand needs to become increasingly associated with usage needs and desires (or 'Category Entry Points') to drive growth. This could be measured via a survey in an unprompted way (e.g., "What brands can you think of that fill you up when you're hungry?") or by using a prompted list of brands (e.g., "Which of these brands fill you up when you're hungry?"). What's important is how the brand's share of mentions increases over time until it 'owns' the dimensions it plans to dominate, thereby growing its 'Mental Market Share.'

During the defensive phase, most of the target audience is aware of the brand and what it stands for, so the priority is to maintain consideration by continuously reminding people about the brand and keeping it salient. For sustained success, brands need to continue matching user expectations as they expand their user base. The net promoter score (NPS, see Section 2.5) is a popular way to measure user satisfaction.

In most categories, people's attitudes to brands change slowly. It can take years for emerging brands to challenge established players, so brand progress can be evaluated annually. For new brands or rapidly evolving categories, however, the brand's standing should be reviewed every six months or quarterly, and systems should be put in place to detect changes in brand performance versus competitors on a monthly or weekly basis. In categories where consumers tend to research their purchase, the number of search queries featuring the brand name is an ideal way to measure how the brand stacks up to competitors. Google Trends provides this data free of charge.

8.3 MEASURING COMMUNICATIONS EFFECTIVENESS

Measuring communications effectiveness requires the extra profit generated by the communications to be compared with the cost of delivering it. Adding up the costs is fairly straightforward but isolating the sales contribution of communications from other variables, including price promotions and competitors' activities, can be difficult. Sophisticated modelling is needed to disentangle the effects and, for multimedia campaigns, tease out the contributions from individual channels.

Sales modelling has shown that some forms of communication, such as TV and magazine 'brand development' advertising, affect sales for an extended period of time, provided they are memorable. This means that focusing only on immediate sales effects would underestimate the value of the activity. In fact, the eventual gain can easily be two to five times greater than the short-term effect. For producing a quick boost in sales, promotional activity is a better bet than brand development communication, although it is unlikely to be of lasting benefit to the brand.

SHORT- VS LONG-TERM RETURN FROM ADVERTISING

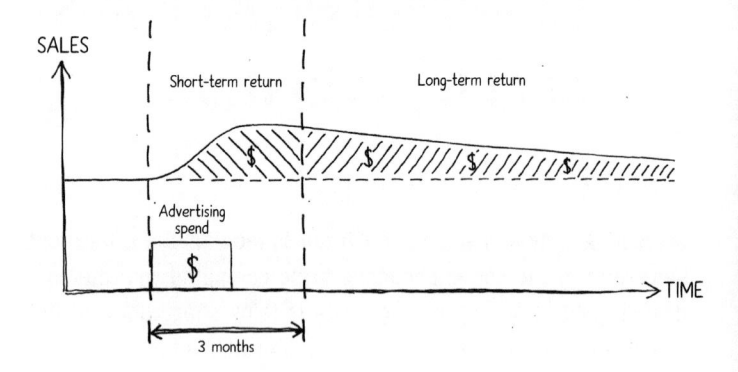

Quantifying the sales impact of communications accurately will not always be viable, but there are ways to check that a wave of communications is being noticed by consumers and to compare the impact with previous waves. A reliable indicator of communications effectiveness is the uplift in the number of people who remember seeing or hearing about the brand recently, measured via a survey. The boost in searches containing the brand is a good alternative in some categories. If the brand spends continuously on communications, uplifts won't be apparent, and more sophisticated approaches such as attribution modelling are needed.

IMPACT OF CONTINUOUS ADVERTISING

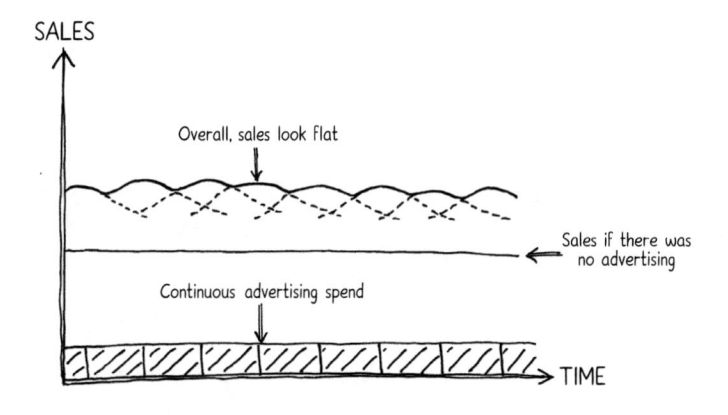

Overall, sales look flat

Sales if there was no advertising

Continuous advertising spend

In markets with lots of activity, communications investment may be necessary just to maintain a brand's sales. If this is the case, the communications can be considered effective if the brand can be maintained with a share of category spend similar to or lower than its share of market.

For brands that spend heavily on communications, knowing if and when to make a fundamental change to the communications can be challenging. There are benefits to maintaining a consistent style of advertising over time, which means that once an effective campaign has been developed, it's worth sticking with it. Coca-Cola's Christmas advertising featuring a cavalcade of trucks has been running since 1995. Familiarity builds trust and repetition helps to create strong memories, so having a common thread running through the communications increases their effectiveness. For more than

20 years, the male grooming brand Axe (Lynx in some countries) based its communications around the idea of giving ordinary young men confidence in dating, conveyed in a tongue-in-cheek style. The 'Axe Effect' campaign was used in many ways over the years to launch new products and fragrances, but never strayed from the winning formula.

Most campaigns, however, have a shelf life. There are three main reasons for changing a brand's communications idea: not right for the times, ideas have dried up and a brand needs to change direction.

REASONS FOR DEVELOPING A NEW COMMUNICATIONS IDEA

NOT RIGHT FOR THE TIMES	IDEAS HAVE DRIED UP	BRAND NEEDS TO CHANGE DIRECTION

NOT RIGHT FOR THE TIMES
Over the long term, a campaign may become outdated. In 2016, Axe moved away from the Axe Effect because it was felt to be inappropriate given changing attitudes to relationships and dating.

IDEAS HAVE DRIED UP
In some cases, the creative team can no longer come up with interesting ways to bring the idea alive. If so, the new communications can be given a head start if they retain strong elements from the previous campaign, such as a character, a graphical element or sonic motif, especially if they have already become strongly linked with the brand.

BRAND NEEDS TO CHANGE DIRECTION
A new communications idea is also needed for repositioning a brand but, even then, existing elements could be incorporated to help people connect the new campaign with the brand – a challenge new campaigns often struggle with. In the 1960s, the Esso tiger was used to represent the potency of the brand's petrol – they suggested putting 'a tiger in your tank.' But in the mid-1990s when price competitiveness became the brand's main focus, the tiger was shown using its night vision to check competitors' prices so that for Esso could match them every day.

8.4 MEASURING CUSTOMER EXPERIENCE

Improving the customer experience has been shown to increase customer retention and revenue per customer while enhancing brand perceptions. This is how customers become fans who come back time and again and recommend the brand to others.

Customer experience can be measured at the following three levels.

MEASURING CUSTOMER EXPERIENCE

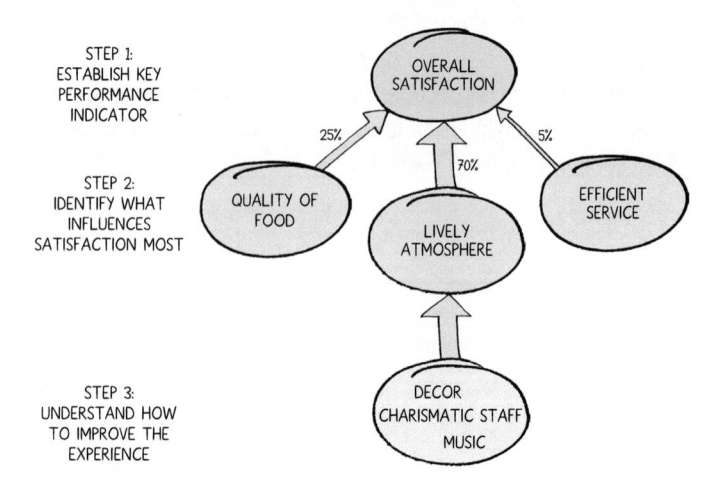

STEP 1:
ESTABLISH KEY PERFORMANCE INDICATOR

STEP 2:
IDENTIFY WHAT INFLUENCES SATISFACTION MOST

STEP 3:
UNDERSTAND HOW TO IMPROVE THE EXPERIENCE

- OVERALL SATISFACTION
  - QUALITY OF FOOD — 25%
  - LIVELY ATMOSPHERE — 70%
  - EFFICIENT SERVICE — 5%
- LIVELY ATMOSPHERE
  - DECOR
  - CHARISMATIC STAFF
  - MUSIC

STEP 1: ESTABLISH KPI
Businesses typically use a rating of overall satisfaction or the net promoter score (NPS) as their key performance indicator (KPI). Both measures are obtained from surveys among a cross-section of customers. NPS is based on asking customers how likely they are to recommend the brand using a scale from zero to ten. The score is calculated by taking the percentage of promoters (scores of nine or ten) and subtracting the percentage of detractors (scores of zero to six). NPS has been thoroughly validated against commercial outcomes and is widely used. Measures of overall satisfaction tend to evolve slowly, so while they could be measured continually, a quarterly or annual review is usually sufficient.

STEP 2: IDENTIFY WHAT INFLUENCES SATISFACTION MOST
The next level of measurement is to identify which aspects of the customer experience have the greatest impact on overall satisfaction. This can be done by asking consumers why they gave a high or low overall score or by obtaining ratings for different elements of the experience and inferring their importance via analysis.

STEP 3: UNDERSTAND HOW TO IMPROVE THE EXPERIENCE
To understand what's expected from an experience and how well the brand lives up to this, customers can be intercepted soon after the experience and asked to complete a short survey. The survey typically assesses the customer's level of satisfaction with that specific interaction and captures any positive or negative comments about it. Examples of this include feedback forms given to guests at the end of a hotel stay, emails or calls after a home installation, pop-ups as people leave a website and texts as people leave a store.

In addition to information about experiences collected via survey, businesses can also measure whether they are meeting service-level benchmarks such as completing jobs or responding to calls within a certain time frame or the time taken to complete a transaction on a website or app. This data can be related to satisfaction levels to determine the variables that affect customers most.

8.5 KEEPING TABS ON THE COMPETITION

The best time to keep an eye on potential threats is when the brand is apparently in great shape. Reacting when the brand is already showing signs of weakness may be too late to prevent long-term decline, so it pays to put a simple, ongoing early warning system in place.

Competitors with a similar profile are, of course, the ones requiring closest attention, especially if they have a lower price, but any brand with an innovative approach to marketing should also be considered a potential threat.

IDENTIFYING COMPETITIVE THREATS

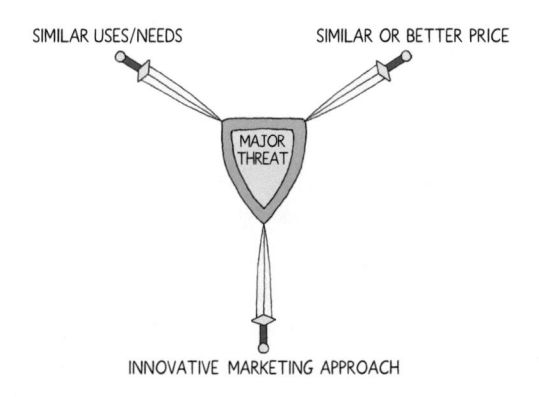

SIMILAR USES/NEEDS

SIMILAR OR BETTER PRICE

MAJOR THREAT

INNOVATIVE MARKETING APPROACH

The rapid growth of computer manufacturer Dell was thanks to a business model that differed from the big established brands. Dell assembled the machines after customers had specified what they wanted and had paid for the order. This created cost and cash-flow benefits and meant the products were better tailored to customers' needs and lower in price. A reliable way to identify brands with major growth potential is to compare their share of consideration measured via a survey (or share of interest measured via search levels) with their share of market.

BRANDS PUNCHING ABOVE THEIR WEIGHT

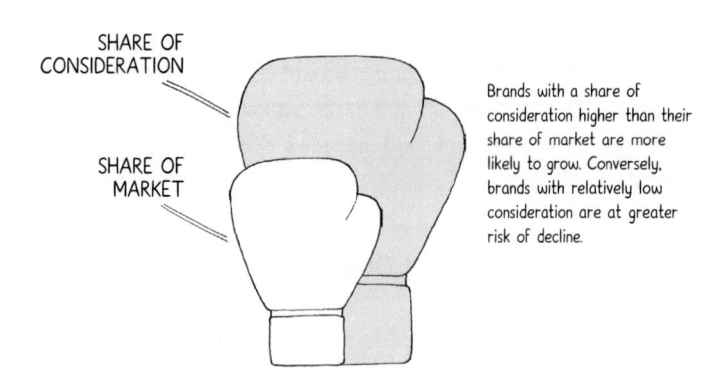

SHARE OF CONSIDERATION

SHARE OF MARKET

Brands with a share of consideration higher than their share of market are more likely to grow. Conversely, brands with relatively low consideration are at greater risk of decline.

A high ratio means people are interested in buying the brand but haven't done so yet, either because the brand is very new or because it's not yet widely available. Such brands tend to grow and could be a major threat if they have the resources to expand distribution and invest more in sales activation to convert interest into actual purchasing. Tesla is an example of a brand that had very high consideration compared to its share of market in its early days. As the brand expanded its distribution and introduced a new, lower-priced model, its high level of predisposition fuelled sales, helping Tesla become one of the world's best-selling brands of car.

If search levels are meaningful in a category, Google Trends can be used to monitor interest in all brands, big and small, so that any emerging threats can be spotted early. Alternatively, survey-based 'brand tracking' could be used. This involves selecting a handful of close competitors and suspected threats and measuring levels of awareness, consideration and purchasing on a regular basis, and imagery on an occasional basis.

PART NINE

IDENTIFYING THREATS & OPPORTUN[ITIES]

- SOCIAL
- TECHNOLOGICAL
- ECONOMIC
- ENVIRONMENTAL
- LEGAL

BRAND REVIEW

9.1 REVIEWING BRAND STRATEGY

Brand strategies should be designed with long-term growth in mind. Assuming the strategy was well thought through in the first place (see Section 2.2), it should remain in place until there is evidence to show it is no longer effective. Most companies scrutinize brand strategy on an annual basis. This involves an assessment of the performance of the brand in terms of sales, consumer predisposition and effectiveness of marketing activity. A strategic review also requires an analysis of any competitive threats and changing consumer priorities.

REVIEWING BRAND STRATEGY

ASSESS PERFORMANCE & TRENDS

- GROWTH ON TARGET
  - NO THREAT ON HORIZON → OPTIMIZE EXECUTION
  - THREAT ON HORIZON → DEVELOP NEW STRATEGY
- GROWTH BEHIND TARGET
  - STRATEGY BEING WELL EXECUTED → DEVELOP NEW STRATEGY
  - STRATEGY BEING POORLY EXECUTED → IMPROVE EXECUTION

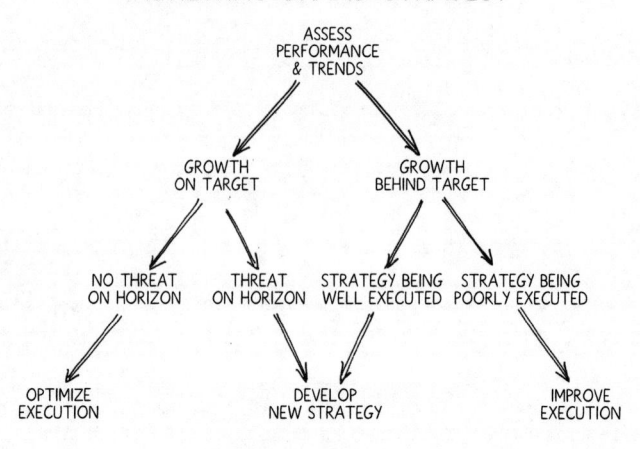

The most important outcome of a brand strategy review is clarity on whether the current strategy will deliver long-term success for the brand. If the brand is continuing to meet targets and no threats have been identified, the brand can focus on keeping up the good work and executing the strategy as cost efficiently as possible.

If the brand is doing well but there is a threat on the horizon (see Section 8.2), the strategy should be evolved so the brand can continue to thrive in the changing market context.

When a brand is struggling to meet targets, the first thing to establish is whether the problems lies with the strategy or its execution. If the strategy has been executed according to plan but the brand has not done well, the strategy is probably to blame. If the execution has been weak, the strategy's potential has not been tested so the priority should be improving the quality of the marketing activity.

If a new brand strategy is required, however, the marketing team needs to go back to first principles and establish what consumers will be looking for in the years ahead and how the brand could provide something uniquely valuable to them.

9.2 DEVISING A NEW BRAND STRATEGY

Development of a new strategy is a three-step process.

The first step is to establish strengths and weaknesses. The most effective strategies are based on the strengths of the brand and company, and don't allow the brand's weaknesses to get in the way of success. Even if a brand has all the same benefits as when it was launched, these historic strengths may have become less relevant as the market developed. Market research is essential for obtaining an up-to-date picture of what people want from the category, what they value most about the brand and what sets it apart from others.

The second step is identifying external threats and opportunities. The STEEL (Social, Technological, Economic, Environmental and Legal) framework is a variant of the PEST (Political, Economic, Social and Technological) framework devised by business strategist Francis Aguilar in the 1960s, designed to help organizations consider the external factors that could help or hinder future success.

IDENTIFYING THREATS & OPPORTUNITIES

SOCIAL

TECHNOLOGICAL

ECONOMIC

ENVIRONMENTAL

LEGAL

SOCIAL
Social factors include changes in the demographic profile of the population that could affect business. An aging population, for example, is good news for healthcare providers. Trends in social attitudes and priorities are also important. An increase in concern for the environment, for instance, leads to greater demand for products and services that don't damage the planet.

TECHNOLOGICAL
New technologies often present threats or opportunities. They could lead to faster, easier or better alternatives, so brands need to keep tabs on relevant, emergent technologies and monitor closely what competitors are experimenting with.

ECONOMIC

Economic conditions can also affect a brand's fortunes. When the economy is struggling, luxury categories and brands tend to suffer, commodities remain unaffected and budget brands tend to thrive.

ENVIRONMENTAL

Environmental changes affect the availability and cost of raw materials and this has a knock-on effect on brand performance. For example, changes in climate can affect crop yields and the cost of ingredients for food products that could, in turn, affect prices, sales and profit margins.

LEGAL

Legal changes can directly affect a brand's options and financial situation. In 2018, the UK government introduced a tax on soft drinks containing sugar. This led to new pricing and distribution strategies for high- and zero-sugar products, which affected the profits generated by the manufacturers involved.

The final step of strategic development is to find an effective growth strategy. A good way to stimulate ideas is to cross-reference the strengths, weaknesses, opportunities and threats from steps one and two using the 'SWOT/TOWS' (Strengths, Weaknesses, Opportunities and Threats) framework.

SWOT/TOWS FRAMEWORK

	OUR STRENGTHS: 1. 2. 3. 4.	OUR WEAKNESSES: 1. 2. 3. 4.
OPPORTUNITIES from external changes: 1. 2. 3. 4.	To exploit these opportunities we will leverage our strengths as follows:	To exploit these opportunities we will address our weaknesses as follows:
THREATS from external changes: 1. 2. 3. 4.	To reduce these threats we will leverage our strengths as follows:	To reduce these threats we will address our weaknesses as follows:

This analysis focuses attention on what's important but also what's coming up. A great strategy ultimately requires careful thought and creativity. The quality of the strategy will influence the return on investment from all the marketing activity to follow, so it's worth allocating enough time and the right people to the process.

9.3 MARKETING PLANNING

Once the brand strategy is in place and the associated Brand PIÑATA has been produced (see Section 2.3), the next step is to create a marketing plan. Although marketing budgets and plans are adjusted on an ongoing basis as circumstances change, most companies develop a default plan once a year as part of the business planning cycle.

The plan specifies the marketing jobs to be done during the next 12 months, the activities designed to get each job done, the associated costs and expected results.

ANNUAL MARKETING PLAN SUMMARY

MARKETING JOBS TO BE DONE	TARGETS	MARKETING ACTIVITIES	COSTS
e.g. Attract new subscribers by promoting advantages of new gizmo	Increase subscriber base by 20% vs previous year	Magazine ad campaign Feb to July. First month free offer to new subscribers May to Sept promoted via magazines & social media	$XXX $XXX
e.g. Persuade existing subscribers to upgrade to our premium service	40% of subscribers to upgrade by end of year	Emails to subscribers each quarter highlighting the benefits of premium Ads on user portal all year	$XXX $XXX

MARKETING JOBS TO BE DONE
These should be defined in terms of how consumer behaviours need to be influenced. All marketing activities should be designed with a short- or long-term behaviour change in mind.

TARGETS
Targets should be expressed in terms of consumer outcomes and, wherever possible, the financial impact.

MARKETING ACTIVITIES
These are the activities that consumers will be exposed to during the year ahead, spanning the whole marketing mix. These could include product launches and the support they'll receive, price changes, promotions and new distribution channels. Since the

marketing budget is often among the first to be reduced if a company's financial situation deteriorates (see Section 1.5), marketers should make contingency plans indicating which activities they will drop if necessary and which they will protect.

COSTS

These should include all costs associated with each activity, including their development and execution.

9.4 BUDGET SETTING

Like any discretionary investment a company could choose to make, there needs to be a sound business case for marketing expenditure. All companies have a finite amount of money available, so the right allocation for marketing depends on how the expected return on investment compares to other areas of the business, such as staff training or IT.

Estimating the return from marketing investments can be challenging but is necessary for illustrating the commercial value of marketing and justifying its budget. Some marketers are uncomfortable making predictions because there are so many unknowns, but businesses are used to making decisions despite uncertainty. Most chief financial officers are happy to accept assumptions, provided they are supported by a logical rationale.

Here's an example of the kind of calculation that helps marketing to sense-check possible investments and to support business cases for marketing expenditures.

ESTIMATING RETURNS FROM MARKETING

	Q1	Q2	Q3	Q4	Q1	Q2	Q3	Q4	ASSUMPTIONS
ADDITIONAL CUSTOMERS	2,000	1,760	1,550	1,360	1,200	1,050	930	720	Activity in Q1 should reach 20k prospects 10% of those reached typically become customers Average customer retention is 60% over 12 months
PURCHASES PER CUSTOMER	3	3	3	3	3	3	3	3	Existing customers buy 3.2 times per quarter
PROFIT PER PURCHASE ($)	20	20	20	20	20	20	20	20	Current selling price is $42 at 50% profit margin
ADDITIONAL PROFIT GENERATED ($)	120K	106K	93K	82K	72K	63K	56K	43K	

OVER FIRST 3 MONTHS		OVER 2 YEARS	
Additional profit generated	$120K	Additional profit generated	$635K
Cost of activity	$107K	Cost of activity	$107K
Return on investment	1.1	Return on investment	5.9

Notice that the short-term return is small. This is often the case for marketing activities, especially in categories with long purchase cycles such as cars or kitchen appliances. The long-term effects, however, can be significant and easily justify the expenditure so it is important to estimate both the short- and long-term benefits of marketing. The influence of marketing on the price a brand can charge has a huge impact on company profit, so this should always be factored into any estimates.

As mentioned in Section 7.1, according to the *Harvard Business Review* in 1992, a business with average economics will increase its operating profits by 11% with a 1% improvement in price, assuming no loss of volume.

In markets where several brands invest heavily in marketing, a minimum level of spending may be required simply to maintain the brand's position. If the objective is to grow the brand, the level of spending may need to be disproportionately high compared to the brand's size. The grid below shows how spending levels typically relate to a brand's chances of growth.

SHARE OF SPEND VS SHARE OF MARKET

	LOW SHARE OF SPEND VS SHARE OF MARKET	HIGH SHARE OF SPEND VS SHARE OF MARKET
HIGHER SHARE OF SPEND THAN PREVIOUSLY	GROWTH POSSIBLE	GROWTH LIKELY
LOWER SHARE OF SPEND THAN PREVIOUSLY	DECLINE LIKELY	SLOWER GROWTH LIKELY

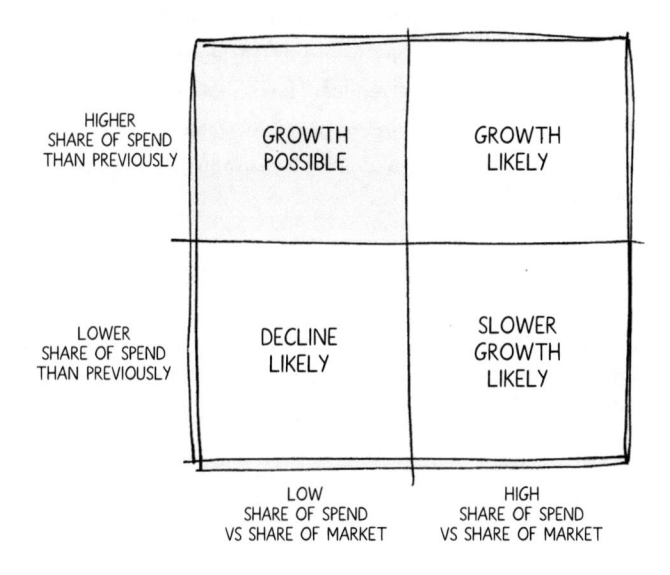

The other major variable is marketing quality. If the brand's strategy is effective and the marketing content is compelling, the brand can achieve growth with much lower levels of spending.

9.5 BRAND PORTFOLIOS

Having a portfolio of brands means a company can generate more revenue while benefiting from efficiencies of scale such as enhanced buying power or reduced innovation costs. The ideal portfolio maximizes the number of people and needs the company addresses while minimizing competition between its brands, also known as cannibalization.

When a new category emerges, one or two brands typically establish themselves and define the category mainstream. Subsequent entrants need to provide a reason to be bought by offering either a premium or budget alternative or positioning themselves as the best at an aspect of delivery that some people value highly.

POSITIONING A BRAND PORTFOLIO

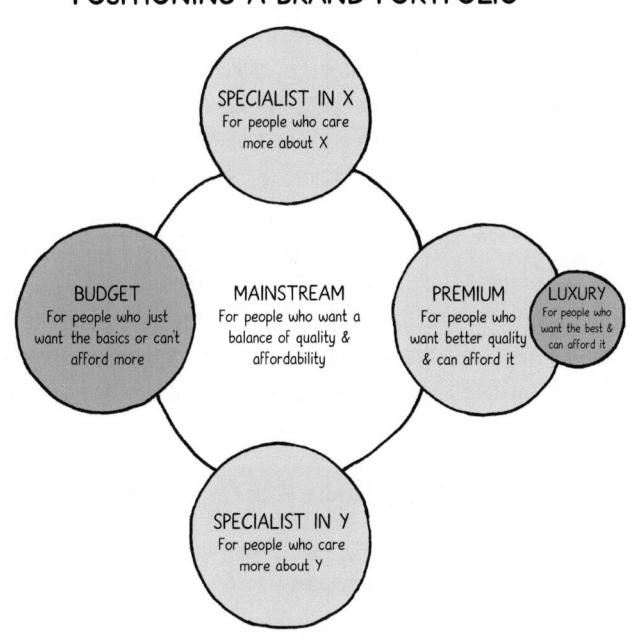

SPECIALIST IN X
For people who care more about X

BUDGET
For people who just want the basics or can't afford more

MAINSTREAM
For people who want a balance of quality & affordability

PREMIUM
For people who want better quality & can afford it

LUXURY
For people who want the best & can afford it

SPECIALIST IN Y
For people who care more about Y

In mature categories, the ideal portfolio has a strong brand in each segment. Automotive giant Volkswagen, for example, has successful brands in the budget, mainstream, premium and luxury segments, i.e., Skoda, VW, Audi, Porsche. This 'House of Brands' strategy means the company can develop brands that appeal to different consumer types and invest profits in whichever brands have the greatest growth potential thanks to their consumer appeal or the growth of their segment.

The alternative is a 'Branded House' strategy in which different sub-brands, under the same 'master brand' name, are positioned to compete in each market segment. Oral care leader Colgate takes this approach. It sells a range of products, each catering to a specific need, e.g., Colgate Regular, Colgate Max White, Colgate Sensitive. This allows the company to build awareness, credibility and appeal in the master brand through all of its marketing. The Dove brand is a good example of how developing a master brand that consumers respect and admire contributes to the success of the whole range.

Brand portfolios allow companies to maximize profit by allocating more budget to brands or sub-brands with the greatest growth potential. In 1970, the Boston Consulting Group introduced a framework to help organizations think strategically about portfolio investments.

BOSTON BRAND PORTFOLIO MATRIX

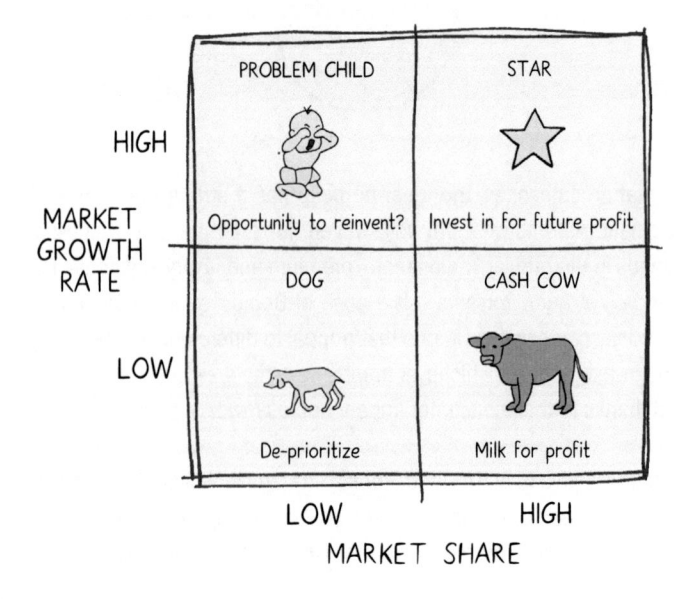

	LOW MARKET SHARE	HIGH MARKET SHARE
HIGH MARKET GROWTH RATE	PROBLEM CHILD — Opportunity to reinvent?	STAR — Invest in for future profit
LOW	DOG — De-prioritize	CASH COW — Milk for profit

The profit each brand contributes today, and in future, may vary enormously. A big, established brand might deliver good profit now, but if the market in which it operates is declining, the profit will dwindle over time. The profit generated by these 'cash cows' should be invested in brands with greater long-term potential such as the 'stars' – brands in a good position within a growing market – so these brands with greater promise can continue to thrive. Alternatively, the money could be invested in 'problem child' brands to help the company capitalize better on the growth of their market. The Boston Matrix also helps identify any 'dogs,' i.e., brands that should not receive any investment because they are struggling versus competitors and are in markets that are unlikely to grow.

PART TEN

BRAND LICENSING AGREEMENT

LICENSING AGREEMENT

BRAND OWNER

Branding rules Pricing rules Approvals

MANUFACTURER

Production Distribution Royalty payment

BRAND EXTENSION

10.1 EXTENDING TO NEW CATEGORIES

Developing a brand in one category can give it a major advantage if it decides to extend into other categories. Brands with a purpose that is relevant outside of their original category, such as Dove's belief in going beyond traditional definitions of feminine beauty, are well placed to extend and enjoy 'halo effects' by which marketing in one category helps sales in all categories. Success in a new category depends on three things.

SUCCESSFUL BRAND EXTENSION

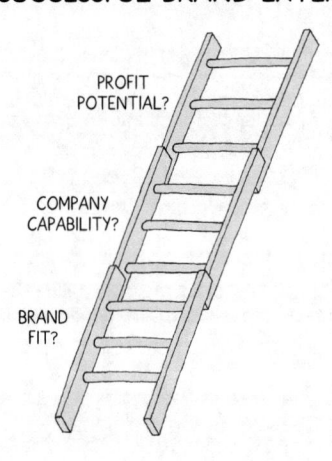

PROFIT POTENTIAL?

COMPANY CAPABILITY?

BRAND FIT?

BRAND FIT

Brands have a head start if the associations they have developed are relevant to the new category. UK fast food chain Leon, for example, has used its distinctive visual style and association with wholesome Mediterranean food to launch a successful range of cookbooks, cookware and tableware products. If the brand's associations are a poor fit, the chances of success are slim. The dental products brand Colgate launched a range of frozen meals in 1982, which did not sell well and were soon discontinued.

COMPANY CAPABILITY

A brand can only extend successfully if the company has the capabilities and resources to deliver a good-quality product in the new category. The viability of a category depends on the time and cost of developing new capabilities or partnering another company.

PROFIT POTENTIAL

The 'Five Forces' framework, developed by economist Michael Porter in the 1970s, helps organizations assess different markets in terms of their potential for making profit.

PORTER'S FIVE FORCES

COMPETITION IS LIMITED

DISRUPTION IS UNLIKELY

DIFFICULT FOR COMPETITORS TO ENTER MARKET

A business has a better opportunity for sustainable profit if...

CUSTOMERS ARE PLENTIFUL

SUPPLIERS ARE PLENTIFUL

A market is attractive if the competition is weak, i.e., there aren't many large companies operating in the market. It has even greater potential if competitors are unlikely to be able to create disruption (for example, by leveraging new technology). Companies also benefit if they have made investments in research and development or in building widespread distribution, making it too expensive for most newcomers to deliver a comparable product.

The potential for profit from a market also depends on the number of potential customers who value the category highly and don't just opt for the cheapest brands. Profits are also higher if there are plenty of suppliers to choose from, and hence competitive prices for essential materials, etc.

10.2 BRAND LICENSING

If a brand has become widely known and popular, it may be in a position to license other companies to develop and sell products using the brand name in return for royalties. Brand licensing allows the brand owner to generate profit from other categories without having to invest time and money developing new capabilities and gives the licensee a way to make its products more appealing to customers. Disney was one of the first companies to license its assets to other companies and continues to boost its profits by allowing third parties to manufacture a wide range of products featuring its brands.

The licensing agreement specifies the responsibilities of each party and the rules each must adhere to.

BRAND LICENSING AGREEMENT

The brand owner defines how the brand should be represented through logos, colours and design guidelines, where it can be sold, how it should be priced and what kinds of price promotion are permitted. The contract also determines the approval process for new products and communications.

When embarking on a licensing programme, brand owners should take care in choosing their partners and establishing reliable procedures for approving how licensees use the brand and checking the quality of what they deliver. Without adequate controls, a brand's identity and reputation could soon be eroded.

Rules about brand communications depend on the terms of the contract. Typically, the licensee is allowed to develop communications designed to promote their product, subject to guidelines and approval from the brand owner. Alternatively, the brand owner may decide to retain complete control over all of the brand's communications.

10.3 SCALING TO NEW REGIONS

Replicating a brand's success internationally can be a great way to multiply its profits. Culture and customs vary across the world, however, so what makes a brand successful in one country does not guarantee success elsewhere. Local brands can tailor their products and communications to the specific mindset and priorities of local people, but international brands can be equally compelling if they have a brand purpose related to a fundamental human need, relevant the world over. Here are some examples in the following illustration.

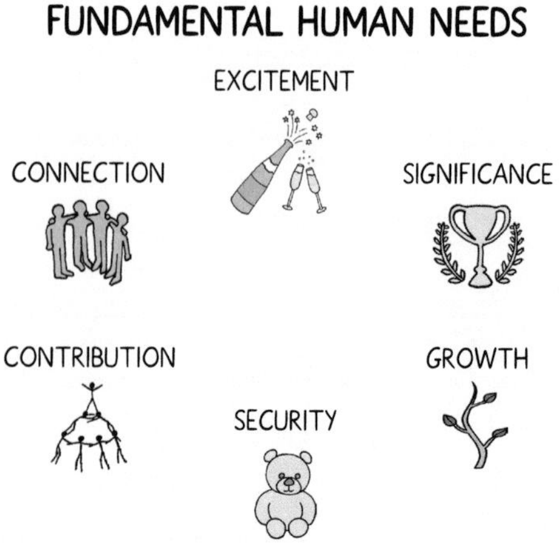

FUNDAMENTAL HUMAN NEEDS

EXCITEMENT

CONNECTION

SIGNIFICANCE

CONTRIBUTION

GROWTH

SECURITY

International brands can also benefit from economies of scale related to production, marketing and innovation, making their products more price competitive and profitable. To realize these efficiencies, international brands need ways of ensuring that brand positioning remains as consistent as possible in all countries so that new products and marketing activities can be shared. From an organizational point of view, a hub-and-spoke model can work well, such as illustrated here.

CENTRAL VS LOCAL MARKETING RESPONSIBILITIES

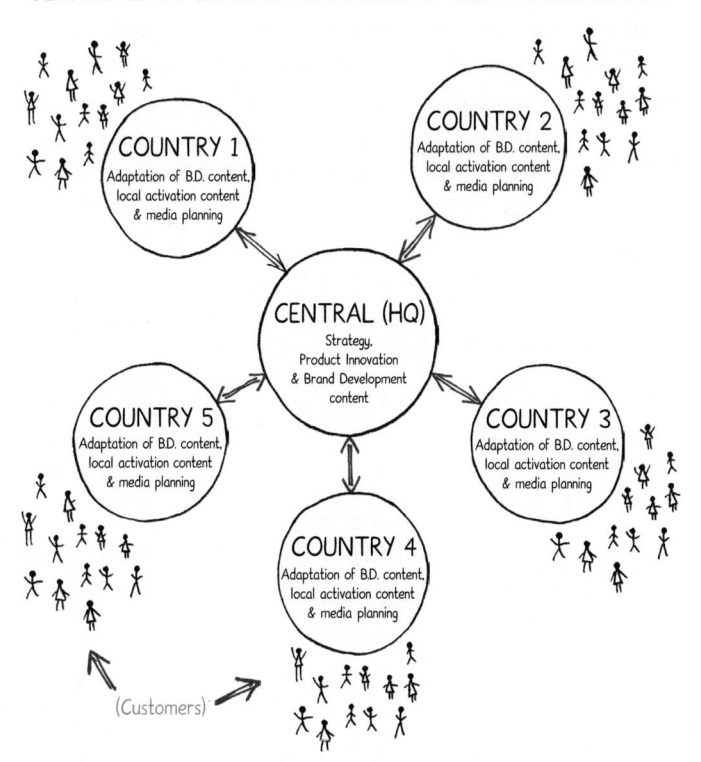

CENTRAL (HQ)
Strategy, Product Innovation & Brand Development content

COUNTRY 1 — Adaptation of B.D. content, local activation content & media planning

COUNTRY 2 — Adaptation of B.D. content, local activation content & media planning

COUNTRY 3 — Adaptation of B.D. content, local activation content & media planning

COUNTRY 4 — Adaptation of B.D. content, local activation content & media planning

COUNTRY 5 — Adaptation of B.D. content, local activation content & media planning

(Customers)

The central marketing function develops the global brand strategy and positioning, leads product innovation and produces brand development content, all shaped by feedback about consumer needs and preferences from the countries. Local teams decide which innovations to launch, choose from or adapt the centrally produced brand development content and develop their own activation content and media plans. This approach creates a lot of efficiency while providing enough flexibility for local teams to optimize the marketing mix for the culture, market context and media environment. A common variation of this model involves having several lead countries that develop innovations and brand development for their country and other countries with similar needs. This means that development is led by teams that are closer to the end consumer and works well if countries fall into obvious groups, which may or may not be related to geography, each with distinct needs.

Regardless of the structure, international brands will be more successful if they have systems in place for countries to share local activation ideas and media plans that have been highly effective so they can be replicated elsewhere.

10.4 INTERNATIONAL VS LOCAL COMMUNICATIONS

Developing communications for multiple countries clearly has cost advantages but isn't always possible. If a brand has grown by launching in more countries over time using the same brand name, proposition and product range, international communications are likely to be effective. If expansion has come from acquiring local brands and gradually migrating them to the global brand, international communications may not be appropriate, especially early on during the transition.

Brands best suited to international communications have four things in common: purpose, usage, brand status and marketing challenge.

BRANDS SUITED TO INTERNATIONAL COMMUNICATIONS

STAND FOR SOMETHING
PEOPLE EVERYWHERE CARE ABOUT

USED IN A SIMILAR WAY
FOR SIMILAR REASONS

COMPARABLE STATUS &
CREDIBILITY VS COMPETITORS

SAME MARKETING CHALLENGE
TO ACHIEVE GROWTH

PURPOSE
The brand's purpose and the consumer insight on which its communications are founded (see Section 2.3) need to resonate with target consumers in all regions.

USAGE
It helps if the brand's products are used in similar ways everywhere. If the category is used differently, communications showing the brand in use will not travel well.

BRAND STATUS
If the brand is highly regarded in one country but lacks credibility in another, the same communications are unlikely to travel well.

Where a brand is unfamiliar, it needs to give people reason to trust and consider it, whereas if the brand is already well respected, it needs to remind people of its strengths and make people feel good about choosing it.

MARKETING CHALLENGE

The role of communications can vary between countries due to differences in where, when and why people buy the category, how it is priced and the competitive landscape. The more similar the marketing challenge, the more likely international advertising will work.

Assuming an international approach makes sense, brands can maximize their effectiveness by finding a communications idea with universal relevance and appeal.

ADVERTISING THAT WORKS INTERNATIONALLY

BASED ON A UNIVERSAL 'HUMAN TRUTH'

USES GLOBAL REFERENCES

ENVIRONMENTS EVERYONE CAN IDENTIFY WITH

LEVERAGES A SHARED BRAND HISTORY

Should've gone to SuperSpex!

A STYLE THAT'S DISTINCTIVE EVERYWHERE

HUMAN TRUTHS
Just as brands based on fundamental human needs lend themselves to international success (see Section 9.3), communications reflecting common human drives are ideal for international brands. Fruitful themes include the desire for adventure, connection with others, sexual attraction, parental love, the search for a soulmate, the wish for a fulfilling old age and the desire to leave a legacy.

GLOBAL REFERENCES
Communications travel well if they leverage cultural phenomena with global appeal such as major sports, popular music, blockbuster movies, human discovery and global internet sensations.

RELATABLE ENVIRONMENTS
Characters, settings and scenarios need to be chosen carefully so they are recognizable and have similar connotations across cultures. One solution is to avoid real-world specifics by creating fictional environments and nonhuman characters that are not tied to a specific cultural context.

SHARED HISTORY
Some communications rely on the consumer being familiar with the brand's previous communications; for example, a running joke. If so, the communications won't be as effective in countries where the brand is new.

DISTINCTIVE STYLE
Communications need to stand out in order to be effective, so for a campaign to travel well, it needs a style that sets it apart regardless of the local norms.

10.5 LEVERAGING YOUR CORE COMPETENCIES

As a brand expands into new categories and countries, the company needs to decide how it wants to manage its growth opportunities.

It could decide to keep everything in-house, developing new capabilities, building relationships with new suppliers and learning about new laws and regulations, but this approach tends to be very slow and highly risky. The most successful companies focus on what they do best and develop partnerships with other companies with expertise in complementary areas. Apple, for example, focuses on developing its core products including personal computers, smartphones, music streaming and app services. It then licenses its brand to external manufacturers to develop and sell a vast range of accessories.

The key to outsourcing is to identify your company's core competencies, i.e., the aspects of business in which you match or surpass other businesses. Your company should keep these areas in-house and ensure that superiority is maintained.

CORE COMPETENCIES

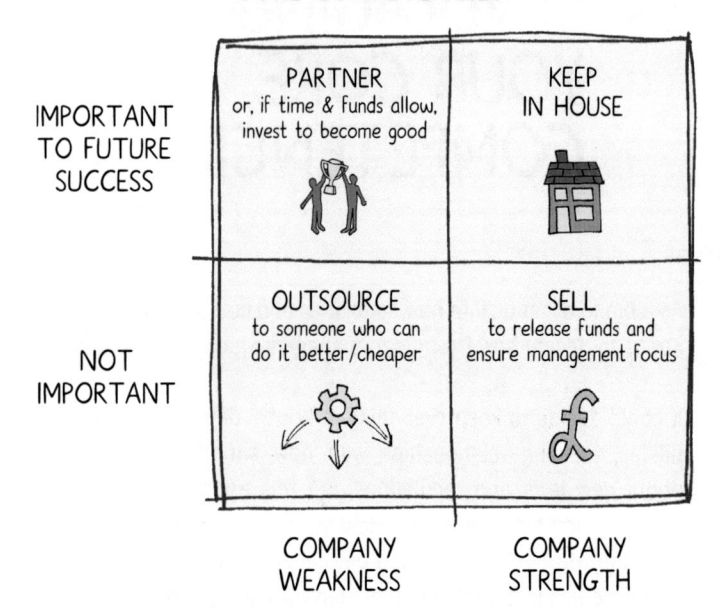

	COMPANY WEAKNESS	COMPANY STRENGTH
IMPORTANT TO FUTURE SUCCESS	**PARTNER** or, if time & funds allow, invest to become good	**KEEP IN HOUSE**
NOT IMPORTANT	**OUTSOURCE** to someone who can do it better/cheaper	**SELL** to release funds and ensure management focus

In all other areas, other options may be better. For example, if an area is important to the business but the company lacks competency in it, suitable partnerships are needed. If there are any areas in which the company is strong but which are irrelevant to future success, the strategy should be to sell what's valuable and reinvest the money in more strategic areas. Areas in which the company is weak and not strategically important should be outsourced to external suppliers better equipped to deliver what's needed at minimum cost.

The key takeaway from this section, and in fact much of this book, should be that a company and its brands must be considered interdependent. Successful companies have a vision for what consumers value, how much they will pay and how much profit this will yield. Brands are simply the mechanism by which the company's vision is made attractive to consumers. Any company that has identified a genuine consumer need and is uniquely placed to address it has an opportunity to generate a healthy profit, but only a smart marketer has the know-how to convert this opportunity into reality.

BIBLIOGRAPHY

Christensen, C., Hall, T., Dillon, K., Duncan, D. "Know Your Customers' Jobs to Be Done." Boston, MA: *Harvard Business Review*, September 2016. https://hbr.org/2016/09/know-your-customers-jobs-to-be-done.

Marn, M., Rosiello, R. "Managing Price, Gaining Profit." Boston: *Harvard Business Review*, October 1992. https://hbr.org/1992/09/managing-price-gaining-profit.

Marn, M., Roegner, E., Zawada, C. "The Power of Pricing." New York: *McKinsey Quarterly*, 1 February 2003. https://www.mckinsey.com/business-functions/marketing-and-sales/our-insights/the-power-of-pricing.

ABOUT THE AUTHOR

DAN WHITE is a marketing and insights innovator. His contribution to the industry includes identifying what makes global advertising effective, scrutinizing the potential for viral, search and 'depth' marketing, and championing innovative marketing measurement techniques.

His frameworks and visualizations have influenced generations of marketers and are built into the world's leading brand measurement, media evaluation and copy-testing systems.

Dan's career includes a decade as a marketing analyst, another as a brand and communications consultant and a third as a chief marketing officer. This unique blend of expertise ensures that every piece of advice offered in *The Smart Marketing Book* is based on robust evidence and a wealth of practical experience.

FROM THE SAME AUTHOR

ISBN: 978-1-911687-70-2

ISBN: 978-1-915951-18-2

ISBN: 978-1-915951-75-5